Jack Russell Terriers

by Deborah Britt-Hay

for
dummies®
A Wiley Brand

Jack Russell Terriers For Dummies®

Published by: **John Wiley & Sons, Inc.,** 111 River Street, Hoboken, NJ 07030-5774, www.wiley.com

Copyright © 2020 by John Wiley & Sons, Inc., Hoboken, New Jersey

Published simultaneously in Canada

For general information on our other products and services, please contact our Customer Care Department within the U.S. at 877-762-2974, outside the U.S. at 317-572-3993, or fax 317-572-4002. For technical support, please visit https://hub.wiley.com/community/support/dummies.

Wiley publishes in a variety of print and electronic formats and by print-on-demand. Some material included with standard print versions of this book may not be included in e-books or in print-on-demand. If this book refers to media such as a CD or DVD that is not included in the version you purchased, you may download this material at http://booksupport.wiley.com. For more information about Wiley products, visit www.wiley.com.

Library of Congress Control Number: 2019952323

ISBN 978-1-119-67563-1 (pbk); ISBN 978-1-119-67564-8 (ebk); ISBN 978-1-119-67561-7 (ebk)

Manufactured in the United States of America

C10015243_110119

Contents at a Glance

Table of Contents

Introduction

I bet you can't turn on the TV without seeing a commercial or a sitcom showcasing the antics of a little dog with crimped ears, an alert expression, and a tail standing at attention.

This saucy little dog has taken the United States by storm and is known as the Jack Russell Terrier or, to those who already own one, a Jack Russell Terrorist. Thanks to the popularity of PBS's *Wishbone* and *Frasier's* Eddie, these British imports have become as hot as the Beatles, Earl Grey tea, and taxation.

WARNING

As a longtime owner and trainer of these remarkable dogs, however, I ask you to take a moment to consider your decision to own a JRT. Yes, they're cute, charming, and very smart. Yes, they're a big dog in a little dog's body and are fun, fearless, and funny to be around. Yes, they're the adorable little white bundles you see plastered on billboards, television, and movie screens. But they also are pushy, are extremely active, and have a voracious appetite for attention. That is why I've written this book — to make sure you're making a well-educated, conscious choice to purchase one of these little white terrorists and to give you the knowledge to keep your sanity after the decision has been made.

About This Book

JRTs, as they are commonly called, aren't for everyone. It takes time, patience, and an unmistakable sense of humor to tolerate their endless antics and tireless energy. For thousands of dog owners across the country, however, no other breed is worth considering.

If you're contemplating buying a JRT, you must first decide whether the breed truly is the right one for you and your lifestyle. These appealing little terriers have complex and distinctive personalities that are significantly different from the Poodles, Dobermans, or Labs with which you may have been raised. This book helps you explore the intricacies — and oddities — of the JRT personality to determine whether you have what it takes to be owned by a Jack Russell Terrier.

After you make your decision, I help you along the fun, but often rocky, path of Jack Russell ownership. You find out about house-training, health issues, typical behavioral hurdles, and how to have lots of fun with your new little soul mate. Along the way, I share some funny stories to show you that you're really not alone in this endeavor and that your terrier isn't that eccentric when compared to other JRTs.

Foolish Assumptions

This book assumes you know nothing about Jack Russell Terriers. If you have some experience with these feisty little dogs, you may want to scan the Table of Contents or Index to determine which chapters relate to your individual situation and interests. If you're considering buying a Jack Russell Terrier, or if you have a new puppy or dog already, this book takes you step-by-step through the fundamentals of raising and training your JRT.

How This Book Is Organized

This book is organized into easy-to-handle parts, each designed to be a mini-book on different aspects of Jack Russell terriers. You can read each part in a short amount of time, without reading other parts. This way, you can pick and choose what you really want to focus on each time you read.

Part 1: Personality Plus! The Basics on Jack Terriers

If you're looking for answers to why your dog does what it does, this part is for you. This part offers explanations for some JRT behavior and what you can expect if you decide to purchase a JRT as a pet.

Part 2: It's All in the Details: Tips for Making the Perfect Match

This part helps you decide which Jack Russell may be the one for you. It offers suggestions on how to find a breeder and how to select a puppy out of a given litter. It also has tips to help you steer clear of potential disastrous situations.

Part 3: Setting Out the Welcome Mat

After you decide on a pup, this part helps you prepare to bring your new family member home. In this part, you discover tips on house-training, puppy-proofing your house, and introducing your new terrier to your existing family members.

Part 4: Creating a Healthy Lifestyle

If you need some information on how to keep your JRT healthy on a daily basis, this part is for you. It covers feeding, exercising, and grooming and gives you tips for keeping your terrier safe, finding a suitable veterinarian, and discovering some fun games to play with your terrier.

Part 5: The Part of Tens

This traditional part of every . . .*For Dummies* book gives you lots of information in a small amount of space. Look here for information on traveling with your terrier, registering your JRT with a club, or visiting great Web sites to get more information than you'll ever need on JRTs!

Icons Used in This Book

Part of what makes this book fun and different from other doggy titles are the icons scattered throughout the book. These small graphics in the margins focus your attention on interesting facts, important information, and safety cautions that can help your training and handling go more smoothly.

This icon highlights special tips for training and caring for your Jack Russell and provide shortcuts that can save you time and frustration.

This icon points out helpful hints that every JRT owner needs to know. Use these to get to know your terrier and to remind you how to approach training your dog.

These icons highlight important health precautions that can save your pampered pooch a lot of discomfort — and save you a lot of sleep. Look here if you think something may be harmful to your dog. This icon also helps you avoid common pitfalls in training, as well as dangerous handling habits that can hurt you or your terrier.

TRY THIS

This icon shows you how to organize your puppy search and perform daily activities with your Jack Russell. If you're looking for things to do with your terrier or need ideas to get you started on a certain training project, look for this icon to get you started.

Where to Go from Here

Not sure where to go next? Here are some tips:

» If you really want a clear road map, start at Chapter 1 and work your way all the way through this book.

» If you're just beginning your Russell search, Part 2 is the place for you.

» If you're having special problems with your terrier, try Part 3.

Remember that you can skip around to the topics that interest you without feeling like you've walked in on the middle of a movie. Each chapter is self-contained.

Beyond the Book

In addition to what you're reading right now, this book comes with a free access-anywhere Cheat Sheet. To get this Cheat Sheet, go to www.dummies.com and search for "Jack Russell Terriers For Dummies Cheat Sheet" by using the Search box.

1

Personality Plus! The Basics on Jack Terriers

Are you considering whether you have what it takes to be owned by a Jack Russell Terrier? If you have it in your mind that the spotted little bundle of joy you pick will grow up to be the next TV star amid the ranks of Wishbone and Eddie, you may be sadly disappointed. Keep in mind that hours upon hours of training have gone into these dogs to make them into trainable little angels. While most JRTs don't approach this level of training, you can find a JRT that will become a cherished pet and important family member, provided you do your homework.

This part explores the JRT personality, discusses typical breed types, and gives you a basic lesson in JRT ownership to help you determine whether a Jack Russell Terrier is the right dog for you or you should begin your search elsewhere.

IN THIS CHAPTER

» Coping with JRT's high energy levels

» Taking a look at inherited personality quirks

» Recognizing some odd but common behaviors

» Sympathizing with the "little dog" complex

» Acknowledging their amazing feats

Chapter **1**

What's a JRT's Temperament Really Like?

I f you've ever spent any time in the company of a Jack Russell Terrier, you know that this little dog is a bit different than any other breed you've encountered. People are drawn to them because they're typically very funny to watch and amusing to be around. Other pets are often puzzled by them because of their boundless energy and their ability to be in a hundred places at the same time.

This chapter identifies the quirky behavior of the JRT and gives you some tips for how to deal with those behaviors.

Talking about Turbo JRTs

One of the most amusing and common behaviors of JRTs is their proclivity for rapid and continuous movement. This can take the form of running at full speed around the house or the yard; through doorways; up and over furniture, b~~~

beings, and other pets; and back the other way like on a makeshift raceway. After a minute or two, they usually stop, grin at you, and then take off again in the other direction. I affectionately call this the *Jack Russell Turbo.*

This behavior shows that the JRT is a high-energy — and high-maintenance — dog. The Jack Russell's energy and exuberance for life can manifest itself in many ways, and turboing is just one of them. Rest assured, yours is not the only household that has been turned into the Indy 500: Jack Russell owners across the nation are befuddled and amused by this sudden burst of terrier energy. If you can get beyond the irritation of being used as part of a pinball machine, you may find this habit rather endearing. If nothing else, it's certain to bring a smile to your face.

TIP

As an added benefit, unwanted houseguests may be quick to change their minds when they get stuck in the middle of the Jack Russell Turbo, leaving you and your family to the relative peace of your home. Granted, you have to take care that *wanted* houseguests are protected from this particular terrier habit.

JRTs TAKE ON HOLLYWOOD

With their spunky personalities, endless energy, and remarkable intelligence, it's no wonder Jack Russell Terriers have become a favorite among producers. From television ads to blockbuster hits, JRTs are making their mark on viewers across the nation. Hollywood and Madison Avenue can't seem to get enough of the Jack Russell Terrier.

More and more JRTs are popping up in the most interesting places — Nissan commercials, ads for the Travel Channel, sitcoms such as *Frasier,* and even a show on PBS called *Wishbone,* in which the big star is — what else? — a Jack Russell Terrier. You may have seen JRTs starring with such film greats as Jim Carrey in *The Mask* and Gene Hackman in *Crimson Tide,* and may have noticed Sparky alongside John Travolta in the angel flick, *Michael.* These little white dynamos are holding their own in the acting department, and I bet they aren't even impressed by the six-figure salaries!

Performing comes naturally to Jack Russell Terriers whether on TV, in the movies, or in your own home. They love to show off their strange and quirky personalities, and they have more than their share of fun while entertaining you and themselves.

In real life, though, Jack Russells are not as they're portrayed in the movies or on television. Don't buy a JRT because you think he's cute or because your children want their own Eddie or Wishbone. In real life, JRTs are nothing like the well-mannered, well-trained stars you see for a few minutes strutting their stuff on television.

Even regular exercise doesn't remove this amusing behavior from your terrier's repertoire, although it may temper it a bit, causing your dog to be a little less rambunctious. If the thought of a little white bullet rocketing through your house at a high rate of speed bothers you, you'll be sorely disappointed in your choice of breeds. Like digging, barking, and hunting, turboing is very much a part of the breed, seen in virtually all JRTs and in all different bloodlines.

Don't leave your puppy alone for extended periods of time unless you want to return home to a demolition derby. Being alone is stressful to your dog.

Observing Forms of Aggression

Although you may normally think of aggression as attacking other pets, dogs, or people (and some terriers can go overboard in this area), the JRT also can exhibit aggression in other, more amusing ways. I know of one dog who attacks the electric garage door every time it's activated. Although this is hilarious to observe the first few times, it can be scary when the little demon forgets to let go and almost gets carried up into the mechanisms of the door. To make matters worse, the dog attacks not only the owner's garage door but any electric door in the vicinity. How do you explain to a neighbor that your dog is defending you from the garage door?

Another story I've heard is about a male JRT who lives on a farm. His favorite pastime is attacking the family's tractor whenever there is work to be done, much to the frustration of the tractor's operator. He growls and attacks the bucket at the front of the tractor, biting the edge and refusing to let go. When that doesn't work, he works his way around to the wheels of the tractor and hangs onto the lug nuts, going 'round and 'round like a slow motion Ferris wheel as the giant tires turn. He does this for hours, obviously convinced in his own mind that he is saving his owners from a ferocious metal beast.

Other aggressive behaviors can take the form of attacking a vacuum, mop, or broom, which can make housecleaning a bit more of a chore than it already is. Some dogs go as far as to actually pounce on the machine and hang on as you try to vacuum, or they grab the bristles of the broom and shake their heads vigorously in an attempt to kill it. Socks and clothes also can fall prey to the ferocious Jack Russell, especially when you're trying to get dressed in the morning and already are 15 minutes late for work. How on earth they know that you're late and need this distraction like you need a hole in the head is anyone's guess, but somehow they manage to choose these times to play! If you can manage it, look at your dog's behavior as a way to lighten up and enjoy the day in spite of your tardiness.

WARNING

Children often assume that, because Jack Russells are relatively small, they should be friendly and easy to hold. And because these types of JRT behavior often are quite funny, your children may be drawn to the dog and want to interact with her. But children should not approach or try to pick up a JRT who displays aggressive behaviors. The terrier becomes somewhat fixated with the object of her attention and, if startled, could snap out reflexively at the child. The dog doesn't intend to hurt the child, but she doesn't make a distinction between the child and the object she's attacking, and she shouldn't be punished if she reacts this way. To the dog, the big bad object would simply be biting back!

Hunting High and Low

Like aggression, the hunting instinct is strongly bred into the Jack Russell, and no amount of training will rid this little dog of her desire to seek out the nearest quarry. Although some terriers are honest-to-goodness rodent hunters and will rid your home, barn, or yard of anything that remotely resembles a rat (like a rock), others use their hunting instincts in a more amusing way.

One of my pet Jack Russells hunts insects on a regular basis. Flies, spiders, mosquitoes — it doesn't matter. He jumps on tables, on couches, in bathtubs — anywhere to gain an advantage over his insect prey. After he catches the bug, he ferociously kills it (which really doesn't take much), proudly leaves it there for all to see, and goes on to his next victim. He stares at the ceiling, the lamps, and the corners of the room to be sure no killer bug has invaded his sanctum. Heaven help the insect that strays into the home of a bug hunter!

Not only will your JRT hunt odd things, she can spend hours doing so. Sometimes she will hunt absolutely nothing at all. One of my best breeding bitches will stare at a hole, corner, or even someone's foot for hours on end, getting up only to feebly scratch at the hole, corner, or foot in question and then sit down and stare again. I call this *gremlin hunting* because only she can see what she's after. At least I know our home is totally free of gremlins!

Examining Random, Nutty Behavior

If turboing and hunting bugs, gremlins, and garage doors aren't bad enough, other even stranger behaviors are considered common within the Jack Russell Terrier breed. Some of these behaviors stem from boredom; others come from an overabundance of energy. All, however, seem to portray the intensity and often obsessiveness of the JRT.

>> **Catching rays:** One of my friend's JRTs goes crazy when her children bring out a flashlight. His favorite game is to play "chase the beam of light." The family turns off all the lights in the room, and the dog goes crazy trying to catch the light spot. Another dog, the product of our own breeding program, goes crazy when his "light saber" (of *Star Wars* fame) is brought out. He runs through the house, jumping several feet off the ground to try to catch the light saber. Another variation of this is a dog who sits by the window every morning waiting for the sun to come up. When the sun rises, it casts shadows on the wall, and the dog spends the next hour or so jumping on the wall to catch the shadows. Sometimes these dogs get so worked up that they have to be put in a crate just to calm down.

>> **Rock dogs:** Rocks also are fascinating to many JRTs. Some carry a rock around for hours and will play "go fetch" with a rock just as they would a ball. Others enjoy chewing or licking rocks — even stalking them. (After all, some rocks can be hard to catch!) Although this habit can be amusing, don't let your JRT get too involved in rock chewing. It can prematurely wear down her teeth, or even worse, it can crack a tooth, resulting in a pretty hefty vet bill to repair the damage.

WARNING

If you find that your terrier is indeed a rock hound, keep an eye on her dental hygiene to make sure she's not severely wearing down the tooth surfaces and that no burrs or debris get caught in the gum, causing possible infection. If you know your dog has had a recent bout of rock wrestling, hold her on your lap and thoroughly check the inside of her mouth — including the inside and outside of the gum surfaces — for abrasions or foreign matter that may have become imbedded. If you find such debris, remove it with a syringe filled with water or with tweezers, much as you would a splinter. Keep an eye on the area for a few days to make sure it doesn't become infected.

TRY THIS

Some dogs choose very large rocks and make digging them out of the ground and rolling them around an all-day project (see Figure 1-1), but your little white terror may get too involved in her digging and end up with a leg or foot injury. Although permitting your terrier to indulge in these activities allows her to burn off pent-up energy, try to limit such physically demanding activities. If you find that your terrier is getting too involved, change her focus by giving her another toy to play with or another activity to divert her attention.

FIGURE 1-1:
Digging in the backyard may seem tame compared to what JRTs can do!

© Tara Darling/AKC Stock Images

A terrier's taste for rocks doesn't always take the form of digging or carrying them. Some Jack Russells prefer to combine their love of rocks with their love of water, making their antics even more amusing. Remember that a JRT is always thinking — some would even say scheming — to find ways to make life more fun and more interesting. What better way to amuse themselves than with their two favorite toys? One of the funniest stories I've heard about JRTs, rocks, and water is about Scooter, a JRT who loves water and jumps in the family pool whenever he's given the chance. One afternoon, after playing with a family member in the yard, Scooter carried the rock he had been playing with into the pool area. There, he accidentally dropped the rock into the pool. As his owners looked on, Scooter leaned all the way over the pool's edge, putting his head under water to try to get his rock back. When this failed, he ran back and forth along the pool's edge barking, trying to bark the rock back up to the surface. After several minutes of futile barking, Scooter tried another plan. He took several steps back away from the pool's edge and jumped head-first into the pool. Ducking his head under water, he literally dove to the bottom of the pool and retrieved his favorite rock. After he taught himself how to do this, "rock diving" became a favorite pastime. Now he often amuses himself for hours by tossing in a rock and going to retrieve it.

Pools aren't the only water sports that JRTs enjoy. One of my dogs, Annie, is a sprinkler fanatic, and this special pleasure is passed down from generation to generation of her puppies. I try to warn new JRT owners about this particular penchant for water, though some fail to realize the extent of the fascination until they experience it for themselves. Many Jack Russells attack yard sprinklers or any human being with a hose in their hand, and try to bite the stream of water that comes out. Some jump several feet off the ground to grab the water, snapping their jaws in a futile attempt to capture the elusive sprays. The best part is the dreamy look on their faces as they smile at you, soaked from head to toe and panting heavily. How could life get any better?

» **Problem solving:** Jack Russells are almost uncanny in their ability to problem-solve, not only with rocks and water but with life in general. Many owners underestimate the jumping ability of their Jack Russell Terriers and are amazed when they find that JRTs jump onto kitchen counters to retrieve a steak left out to thaw or a cookie out of the cookie bin. They also are clever about finding their way into backpacks, duffel bags, and drawers, especially if their keen noses pick up something that smells delectable. I have known JRTs to unzip zippers with their teeth, to open drawers with their front paws, and to undo seemingly impossible clasps to get to the desired treat. If you own a JRT, take a word of advice — never underestimate the tenacity of a Jack Russell!

» **Tasting the furniture:** Another odd behavior common to JRTs is the desire to lick a certain piece of furniture whenever the dog becomes excited. The object might be the corner of a bookcase or the side of a bathtub. Why they do it is anyone's guess, but like all their obsessions, they focus on the object with fierce determination and can literally lick the finish off of the furniture.

I know from personal experience that hot sauce, cayenne pepper, and the like aren't deterrents when a terrier sets her mind, or in this case her tongue, to a task. The only way to stop the behavior is to catch the dog every time you see her licking the furniture and tell her "No!" Usually the dog is stimulated by your presence, such as when you first come home, so she only exhibits this behavior in front of you. The fact that you're there to watch makes it easy to modify the behavior. (Other behaviors, such as digging or hunting rocks, usually are done for the dog's own amusement while you're away; however, they are no less frustrating.)

If you don't have a sense of humor about such things, don't purchase a Jack Russell Terrier. Like the changing weather and the tides, some things just can't be stopped, and a terrier's odd behavior is one of them. You may be able to get your dog to decrease the frequency of some of her less-desirable idiosyncrasies, but some will always remain.

» **Break-dancing:** That Jack Russell Terriers love to sleep on their backs with all four feet in the air is pretty common knowledge, but did you know they also incorporate this position into another quirky behavior I affectionately call *break-dancing?* It's true. One day, an unsuspecting JRT owner will walk in and see his little white terrorist on her back dancing across the floor. Some seem to do it as a form of scratching the itch on their backs. Others do it when they're excited, such as when their owners get home after an absence. Whatever the reason, the first time you see it, you'll undoubtedly do a double take. You may also find a nice patch of white hair on your carpet when your funny friend is done dancing.

Some dogs wiggle up and down, back and forth like a sidewinder rattlesnake. Others stand with their rears in the air and their tails wagging as they rub their heads all over the carpet before blissfully throwing themselves to the ground and rubbing their entire bodies on it. Either way, it looks rather odd. What's even funnier is hearing embarrassed owners trying to explain their dog's behavior to their houseguests. Of course, anyone who owns a JRT soon gets used to this kind of embarrassment.

Understanding the Napoleon Complex

Perhaps one of the most prevalent oddities of the Jack Russell breed is the dogs' obliviousness to their size. Any Jack Russell owner can tell you that their tiny terrorists view themselves as bigger than a Rottweiler and twice as mean. Although "feisty" is one of the most common words used to describe a Jack Russell Terrier, no one really knows the true accuracy of this description until they have spent some time in the company of a JRT when she's around a larger dog. The comedy is revealed when, inevitably, the larger dog backs down in the face of the ferocious white whirlwind.

Although many novices assume on first glance that this bravado is a bluff to get the larger dog to back down, those who know the breed understand that nothing could be further from the truth. A JRT truly believes she's as large as and twice as mean as the dog she's approaching. Although this ferociousness may catch the larger dog off guard, causing it to flee rather than to fight, many Jack Russells have gotten themselves into serious trouble by picking a fight with a larger, meaner dog and not knowing when to quit. Being no real match for a dog the size of a Rottweiler, the JRT can quickly end up on the losing side of the battle. Worse yet, she may refuse to give up until she's virtually torn to pieces.

You need to be your JRT's guardian in these circumstances and not allow her to be overmatched to the point of being injured. If you know that another dog is likely to be aggressive or will defend herself rather than back down, protect your terrier from her own bravado. Either pick your dog up until safely out of the other dog's reach or give the other dog a very wide berth. The saying is true — a JRT often is her own worst enemy.

Jack Russell Terriers often are referred to as "the big dog in a small dog's body." Ironically, JRTs get along much better with larger dogs than they do with smaller ones, perhaps because of their inflated self-image.

Admiring Their Amazing Feats

Although Jack Russell Terriers behave oddly at times, they also possess an almost uncanny ability to notify their owners when something is amiss. Countless stories have been told about JRTs who have saved a child or another pet from injury or have alerted their owners to a dangerous situation.

One such instance was related to me by the owner of a JRT who had been raised from puppyhood with a cat whom she considered to be a friend. One day, after moving to a new home, the owner came home to find the cat missing and the back door ajar. The owner searched around the back of the house to no avail. During her search, her JRT named Max kept running up to her, putting his front paws on her legs and then running in front of her and looking back. Irritated by the distraction, the owner kept chasing the terrier away and calling the cat's name.

Finally, she gave up and went back in the house. She sat down by the phone, intending to call some friends to help her search for her cat. The moment she sat down, Max jumped onto her lap and then immediately off again, took several steps away and looked back at her. This happened several times before she finally decided to follow him and see what he wanted. Max dutifully led her into the woods to a large, gnarled stump about 400 feet from her house. She looked inside the opening, only to find her cat, who had been hit by a car. She rushed the kitty to the vet, who said that, had she waited much longer, he would not have been able to save the cat.

Another amazing story also involves a JRT and her kitty pal. Shilo and her cat buddy, Boots, were out in the driveway sunning themselves on a particularly warm fall day. When the sun got too hot, Boots decided to curl up under the shade of the family's car. Unbeknownst to the family, the cat climbed into the car's undercarriage and fell asleep. When the owner came out to run to the store, the cat was stuck under the car. Rather than let her little friend become mincemeat, Shilo barked and ran behind the car, preventing the owner from backing out of the driveway. When the owner got out to see what the fuss was about, he realized that the cat was stuck under the car and couldn't get out. After some wiggling and twisting, Boots was freed unharmed. Who says JRTs and cats can't get along?

If, after reading this chapter, you're convinced that you're ready to take on this little dynamo, the next step is to decide which JRT is right for you. If you still are doubtful after these stories of antics and heroics, do yourself a favor and explore some other breeds. You have to be 100 percent sure of your decision if the relationship is going to work. If you have any doubt in your mind, either spend some time around a Jack Russell Terrier to see whether you have what it takes to be owned by one or pass on purchasing a JRT until you're in a position to take on the responsibility. JRTs aren't easy dogs to live with, although they do make amusing housemates.

Chapter **2**

The Telltale Signs of a Jack Russell Terrier

To determine what's "correct" in terms of *conformation* (the structure of the dog), you first must understand the characteristics that are considered "accepted breed standard." This concept may be harder to answer than you think. Due to the split between the American Kennel Club (AKC), the Jack Russell Terrier Club of America (JRTCA), and the Jack Russell Terrier Breeder's Association (JRTBA), and because of the further addition of the English Jack Russell Terrier Club of America (EJRTCA), the matter of "standard" becomes somewhat blurred because each registry holds its own specifications as to desired type. The AKC is not currently accepting applications for new registrations and the EJRTCA focuses only on the newer, short-legged type of dog, so this chapter examines the JRTCA standard and how it may apply to your dog search.

TIP

If you're confused, you're not alone. Like any dog, the JRT has become the victim of fads and personal preferences. This chapter focuses on the requirements for the JRTCA registry. Some of the requirements for this registry are similar to the requirements for other registries; other requirements vary widely. What really matters is that if you choose to become involved in a registry, you want to know what's expected of your terrier's conformation. If you simply want a great pet, most of these do's and don'ts won't concern you too much.

NOT YOUR AVERAGE HISTORY LESSON

Like many historical beginnings, the breed known as the Jack Russell Terrier began as a quest — in this case, a quest for a better hunting dog. The story began somewhere between 1815 and 1820 with an avid fox hunter, Reverend John Russell, the vicar of Swimbridge in Devon, who decided he wanted a more efficient fox-hunting terrier than those found within the local dog population. Rather than search the world over to find the perfect hunting companion, Parson Jack, as he was affectionately known, decided to take the best dogs he could find in his area and breed exactly the type of terrier he sought. Thus, the first Jack Russell Terriers were born.

The original female (or *bitch,* to use the proper breeding term) was a terrier named Trump. The vicar found Trump in Oxfordshire while attending Exeter College at Oxford. He immediately was struck by her stature and markings and by her resemblance in size to the vixens he so often hunted. Trump was considered the foundation terrier in Reverend Russell's breeding program and has now become a legend in Jack Russell history. In fact, her likeness still adorns the entrance to the Jack Russell Inn, which is near Barnstaple in England.

Stories say that Trump was predominantly white, with only a patch of tan over each eye and ear (also called a *full mask*) and a penny-sized dot at the base of her tail. Her coat was wiry, and her body was strong and sturdy. She was between 13 and 14 inches tall and possessed all the traits Parson Jack had been looking for in a hunting dog. After some tough negotiating, he made a deal with the milkman who owned her, and Parson Jack happily became Trump's new owner.

Parson Jack preferred mostly white terriers with few markings and strove to produce dogs with these characteristics. In spite of his preference for white coats, however, the first mating is thought to have occurred between Trump and a fine young terrier with a black-and-tan broken coat. The resulting litter created history as the foundation stock for the Jack Russell type of terrier.

By the 1850s, Parson Jack was considered one of the leading breeders of terriers in England. By the time he died at age 88, Reverend John Russell had made a significant mark on fox-terrier history. Allegedly, his breeding stock was disbursed upon his death to Squire Nicholas Snow and, eventually, to Arthur Heinemann, who continued to produce quality terriers in the type and style of Parson Jack's dogs.

Looking for Perfection

Like it or not, no dog (or dog owner for that matter) is perfect — all have one fault or another. In Jack Russell Terrier terms, several characteristics are considered breeding faults and are penalized in show competition. Any dog displaying shyness, overaggressiveness, or disinterest is penalized. It's hard to be a big game hunter when your dog is snoring under a bush or attacking other dogs! Likewise, a dog who runs at the sight of a fox hardly is considered an asset.

Hunting faults

The list of physical faults is quite long, and any trait considered weak for hunting is penalized. These necessary characteristics are crucial because a dog's success during the hunt depends on his ability to maneuver and to physically perform the tasks asked of him.

WARNING

The terrier must be able to be heard when below ground, so a strong voice is important. Without it, the dog could be hidden in a hole while his owner searches futilely to find him. Although the bark should be easily heard, it shouldn't be high pitched or shrill. You will recognize this fault right away the first time you hear it. A shrill voice penetrates your skull in much the same way as fingernails on a chalkboard. Your only goal in life becomes to find some way to make him stop!

Specific physical flaws

The dog must be in fit condition without physical characteristics to hinder him in his work. To this end, the following are considered to be extensive physical faults:

- Weak or undermuscled jaws
- Incorrect bites
- Thick or fat ears
- Shoulder blades that aren't well formed or that dip down significantly behind the base of the neck
- Narrow or weak hips that could lead to hip dysplasia
- Ribs that are too sprung, causing a barrel-like appearance
- Legs that bow out at the knees *(bull-legged)*
- Legs that are too straight between the top of the hind leg and the hock (the knee-type joint on the back legs)
- Small or weak feet
- Sluggish or unsound movement
- Toeing out or toeing in, which prevents the leg from swinging in a straight line when the dog walks

- » Flipping of the feet either in or out while walking or running

- » Silky or woolly coats

- » Shrill or weak voices

- » Lack of muscle tone or skin tone

- » Lack of stamina or lung reserve

- » Any evidence of *foreign blood* (a breed other than the standard terrier mix)

Quite a list to say the least! Does this mean that a dog with any of these traits is totally unacceptable? No. It simply means the dog would be considered less than ideal in the conformation or breeding class if you were to present him to a licensed Jack Russell Terrier judge for inspection. Most of these factors wouldn't strongly affect a dog who is a pet, although some could lead to future physical limitations and others, such as the shrill bark, may be quite annoying.

Your personal choice

Most JRTs make wonderful pets, but not all make wonderful show dogs. It's much easier to find a dog of pet quality than it is to find a dog of breeding or show quality. Keep in mind that dogs who are presented in AKC, JRTCA, or JRTBA conformation trials are the only ones judged by these standards, and only dogs who are shown are penalized for these weaknesses. Judge your individual dog by the use you intend for him, and forgive his minor faults if his function is to serve as your companion and lap warmer. Last I checked, JRTCA and AKC had no classes for bed pillows or slipper retrievers.

REMEMBER

Don't allow a breeder to dissuade you from a dog you're drawn to in favor of a more expensive show-quality dog unless you're seriously planning to breed or show your dog. Although the other dog may be more conformationally correct, the most important feature in a pet is personality. Allow your temperament and preference to be your guide.

In the end, it is important to buy from a reputable breeder and to buy the healthiest dog you can find that best fits the criteria you have selected as important. Unless you're planning to show your terrier in conformation classes, forgive weaknesses that are unimportant to you, provided they don't jeopardize the health and future of your pet. Personality, temperament, and appeal are the most important qualities you should consider, and then have your dog spayed or neutered as soon as your vet says it's feasible. Don't fall into the lure of breeding a pet-quality dog just to raise a few bucks. It won't pay off in the long run, and you will be adding to the problems the breed already faces — overpopulation and indiscriminate breeding.

If you do plan to show your dog (see Chapter 14), specifically in conformation classes (remember, working class dogs are judged on their performance, not their conformation), or if you're considering breeding your dog in the future, buy the best dog you can afford with well-known, registered parents and from the most prestigious breeder you can find. If you plan to breed your dog, you have to be even more careful about temperament and have to seek even higher standards in conformation and pedigree.

THE ABCs OF JRTs

The Jack Russell Terrier Club of Great Britain (JRTCGB) was founded in 1975 by Mrs. Romayne Moore, a longtime advocate of the working Jack Russell Terrier and a former founder of the Midland Working Terrier Club. After several false starts and misdirected ambitions, the JRTCGB became the governing body for Jack Russell Terriers in England. This organization is responsible for drawing up breed standards, by-laws, and rules, and it must keep a complete and accurate registry of all eligible Jack Russells in England. It's also responsible for overseeing the future of the breed, including its primary goal of preserving it first and foremost as a hunting dog.

Though a select few terriers may have made their way to the United States earlier, the most significant import occurred when Mrs. Slater offered the gift of a JRT puppy to her friend, Mrs. Crawford, in New Jersey in the 1960s. So taken was Mrs. Crawford with her new dog, named Rare, that she wanted to find out everything there was to know about this curious little dog, such as where the breed originated and how to start a breeding program for them in the United States. She set off for England to educate herself about the breed and its history. Armed with this information, Mrs. Crawford contacted as many experts as possible and purchased several terriers to begin her own breeding kennel in the United States, Hamilton Farm Jack Russell Terriers. Between the early 1960s and 1978, Mrs. Crawford produced some of the top Jack Russell Terriers in the country and made a solid name for herself as one of the foremost breeders of Jack Russell Terriers in the United States.

In 1976, Mrs. Crawford founded the Jack Russell Terrier Club of America (JRTCA). Until recently, the JRTCA was the only registry available in the United States to register Jack Russell Terriers. She also became a judge and is known as the foremost defender of the Jack Russell Terrier as a working dog rather than as a show dog, with all its required characteristics.

Getting Acquainted with the JRT's Characteristics

Before examining the specific physical characteristics that makes this dog unique, I first take a look at the overall appearance that a JRT should present. First, the terrier must appear to be alert and energetic. He also should appear to be quick-witted, should be eager to join the fray, and should be confident in his actions. The dog should appear balanced and square, even at first glance, and should give the appearance of strength and good health. See Figure 2-1.

Because the Jack Russell Terrier was bred to be a hunting dog, he must appear ready for action and excitement and should present a picture of a friendly, outgoing dog with a bright look and a cheerful expression. If you've seen even one Jack Russell Terrier, you've probably noticed that quick, eager-to-pounce look in his eyes, especially if you pick up a ball or another toy. This is the quality that the standard talks about.

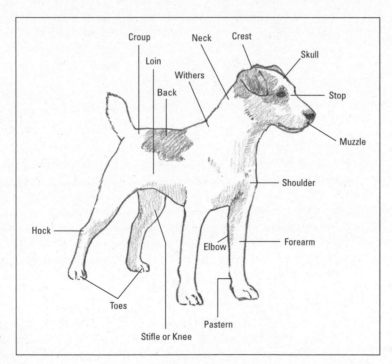

FIGURE 2-1: The anatomy of a JRT.

DIFFERING OPINIONS

In recent history, there has been dissension about the breed standard even between breeders of Jack Russells. For years the JRTCA and the Jack Russell Terrier Club of Great Britain (JRTCGB) allowed a wide range of height and body style standards to allow for the different types of Jack Russell Terriers, although they favored the longer-legged dogs more similar to the originals Reverend Parson bred. In fact, at least two clubs — the Jack Russell Terrier Breeder's Association (JRTBA) and the Parson Jack Russell Club in England — have splintered off from the original registries. Not only do these clubs strongly favor the longer-legged dogs, they also welcome recognition by the American Kennel Club and the English Kennel Club. They are quite pleased by the recent acceptance of Jack Russell Terriers into both kennel clubs, and they are continuing their efforts to build strong relationships with their all-breed cousins.

Because JRTCA and JRTCGB members are adamantly opposed to the kennel club affiliations, it isn't hard to imagine the rift between the two factions. To further muddy the waters, the English Jack Russell Terrier Club of America (EJRTCA) is fighting to uphold the short-legged Jack Russell Terriers and is beginning its own registry for just this type of dog. Now all the registries are preventing cross-registry of any type, creating a serious fragmentation of Jack Russell breeders across the United States and England.

Basic temperament

Although a JRT always should be game for a good hunt, he shouldn't have a hair-trigger bark, shouldn't yap at anything that passes by, and shouldn't appear anxious or nervous. A dog that feels the need to bark at the slightest perceived threat usually is timid by nature, a definite fault in the Jack Russell breed. Any inclination toward cowering, timidity, or nervousness is also undesirable. Even as a pet, you can see why these traits are frowned upon. Because the JRT's bark is quite loud and distinct, you really don't want to be awakened ten times during night because your JRT *thinks* he may possibly hear something as far as ten blocks away.

REMEMBER

Don't confuse nervousness with high energy. A Jack Russell Terrier is always on the move, hunting and exploring his surroundings. An anxious dog — one who routinely paces or is easily upset by changes in his surroundings — isn't considered to be of ideal JRT temperament.

WARNING

Although the Jack Russell should be confident in his actions, overaggressiveness — especially toward humans — isn't a desired trait. The JRT is bred to be confident in his job as a hunter and to either flush quarry out of its den or hold the quarry in the hole until his master comes and calls him off. Except for his job as a rat hunter, the dog isn't asked to attack the quarry, and any such tendencies are seriously frowned upon. As a hunting dog, the JRT should work alongside his master, holding when asked and relinquishing his prey when commanded. He should happily comply with his owner's wishes and should be neither encouraged to display aggression nor punished for being bold.

Intelligence

Along with their alert, energetic appearance, JRTs should also exude intelligence, which they often do to a maddening degree. The dog is quick to solve problems and is eager to find ways around perceived barriers. All this quick thinking makes the dog delightful to be around and humorous to watch. But be careful. Many Jack Russells have been known to outsmart their owners!

Charming and playful, the JRT is happiest in the company of his owner, either snuggled up on a bed or curled up at your feet, but always on the lookout for a good game of ball. Remember, however, that the Jack Russell Terrier is far from a couch potato. He needs regular play periods throughout the day to be truly content.

WARNING

When at a loss for a playmate, the JRT is likely to create his own entertainment, either by tearing through the house at breakneck speed like a drag racer, by teaching himself to sit like a gopher to get your attention, or by barking at you and then running off to try to entice you to play. The bottom line is, you have to have a sense of humor to appreciate a Jack Russell Terrier.

Taking a Look at the JRT's General Appearance

Jack Russells come in all shapes and sizes (see Figure 2-2), but should range in height from 10 to 15 inches at the *withers* (the point between the dog's shoulder blades), and the JRTs legs should be roughly the same length as his body. You'll find a lot of controversy over this wide range of acceptable JRT heights. Such a range was deemed necessary, however, to accommodate the needs of all hunters with varying quarry.

With the exception of the EJRTCA, none of the governing bodies approve of the short-legged JRT because of this dog's inability to easily keep up with horses on the hunt. Opponents also cite another drawback to this style of dog, pointing out that a short-legged dog is stocky in build, which prevents the dog from easily going down to the ground. Because the quarry these dogs seek often lives in dens deep within the earth and because the openings to these dens often are quite small, any dog who may have trouble penetrating these holes is considered more hindrance than help.

FIGURE 2-2:
A group of Jack Russell Terriers sits facing the camera.

Because the dogs were bred to be working dogs, all registries understand that scars or injuries as the result of work or an accident should never be penalized unless they interfere with the dog's movement, utility, or ability to reproduce. Such scars often are seen on Jack Russell Terrier champions and are the result of either controlled hunting or the dog's own hunting excursions.

REMEMBER

When showing Jack Russell Terriers, two groups take into account the wide range in acceptable heights. The smaller class features dogs from 10 to 12½ inches. The taller class allows dogs from 12½ inches up to the maximum of 15 inches in height. Any dog under 12 inches or over 15 inches is not allowed to compete in conformation classes.

Body fundamentals

The dog's body should be in proportion to his height, creating the appearance of squareness. His trunk and legs should be well muscled and solidly fit. Sturdy and tough are words often used to describe a Jack Russell's body type, and the overall appearance should be balanced. In male dogs, both testicles must be fully formed and descended to be eligible for competition.

The chest should be narrow, and the front legs should be set fairly close together (like the body of a competitive diver or an endurance runner). This characteristic enables the Jack Russell to enter the holes of his prey without getting stuck, an important attribute because many dens are quite long and deep — and it's very difficult to dig out a JRT who gets caught within the depths of a foxhole. An age-old guideline is that the circumference of the chest behind the withers can be encircled by average-sized hands when the terrier is in hunting condition. A barrel-chested dog is not able to easily go down to the ground and is considered less than ideal.

Tops and tails

Look for the following characteristics in the head, ears, teeth, neck, legs, and tail:

>> **Head:** The head of a Jack Russell Terrier should be in proportion to his body and should be well muscled through the jaw and the cheeks. He should be moderately wide and should narrow to a clean, fine muzzle. The dog shouldn't have an excessively long nose nor should he appear pug-nosed. The skull should be large enough to enclose a rather large brain, at least in dog terms, but he shouldn't be coarse or heavy. The eyes should be bright and full of life and always should be watching and taking in the dog's surroundings. The eyes usually are dark in color.

>> **Ears:** The ears should be small and should present a V-shaped appearance when held at attention. They should not stand straight up away from the head (prick-eared) nor should they droop or fall heavily from the top. The ears should be relatively thin and well shaped and shouldn't be fleshy or thick in appearance. They should look like little triangular flaps that fall evenly over the ear opening.

WARNING

>> **Bite:** The bite should slightly overlap in a scissor bite and should be strong and well formed. If the dog has a pug-nosed appearance, it could be the result of an incorrect bite. Likewise, a dog who looks buck-toothed probably has an overbite.

>> **Neck and shoulders:** The neck should appear muscular but clean and should taper well into the shoulder, which should be well-laid back and sloping. When looking at the dog from the side, you should be able to see clean, long lines. The angles of the shoulder should look proportional to the angles of the leg, creating a strong, functional front end. There also should be a good angle from the *point of the shoulder* (the point that sticks out in front of the dog's chest) to the *withers* (the point where the two shoulders meet behind the dog's neck).

>> **Front legs:** The terrier's front legs should be straight and strong without any deviation as the leg falls from the shoulder.

>> **Back legs:** The hindquarters should appear muscular and should show good angulation for drive and impulsion. Look or feel with your fingers to be sure the angles of the hind legs have good slope and are easy to flex. A dog with hind legs that are too straight won't have enough impulsion to keep up with running horses and hounds, and his movements will appear more labored.

>> **Tail:** The tail should be set high and carried gaily. It should be *docked* (shortened shortly after birth) long enough to serve as a handle, which is used to pull the dog from the dens he was bred to find. One of the most common mistakes made by veterinarians in the United States is to dock the JRT's tail too short. A good rule is to dock the tail to two-thirds of its original length. If there is a question, the vet should err on the side of leaving it too long. A properly docked tail should look more like a handle than a stub. When shown, however, a dog is not penalized for having too short a tail, provided it is set well onto his body.

REMEMBER

While some people express concerns over the docking of tails, most respected vets concur that if the shortening of the tail is done within the first five days after birth, the trauma to the puppy is extremely minimal. These vets believe that a puppy feels a quick, sharp twinge, similar to a needle prick, and slight soreness for the next 24 hours. After that, he experiences no discomfort at all. It's a minor process and one that the puppy soon forgets. Some countries don't allow docking, however, so be sure to check with your local Jack Russell association before proceeding.

Coat types and colors

Although everyone agrees the Jack Russell Terrier should be predominantly white, markings that are black, brown, and tan are acceptable as long as the coat is at least 51 percent white. Most markings come in the form of masks (dark patches around one or both eyes) and body spots. Some JRTs are marked more brightly, however. All are acceptable, provided the markings don't overpower the basic white coat color. Too much coat coloring (more than 50 percent) and *brindle markings* (layers of black pigment in regions of lighter color) are unacceptable. In fact, a liver nose is a deep reddish-brown color that will disqualify a Jack Russell Terrier from the show ring. (But it won't disqualify a dog from being a great companion!)

There has been much debate over which coat type should be considered desirable. Currently, there are three accepted coat types: smooth, rough, and broken. (Smooth and rough coats are shown in Figure 2-3.)

>> **Smooth:** If smooth, the coat should be thick and dense for protection against the elements and brush, and it should not feel silky to the touch. Many people claim the *shorthaired* (smooth-coated) Jack Russells shed more, but that could be because their coats are a little more dense and there is more hair to lose.

In addition, the shorter hair seems to work its way more easily into the fibers of your clothes, especially whenever you choose to wear black. The best solution is a good brush that you use often and a good vacuum cleaner.

>> **Rough:** Rough-coat dogs often appear wiry. The rough-coat dog requires regular *stripping* (a deep-down grooming that loosens dead hair and removes them from the dog's coat) to maintain a neat appearance, although all coat types require some degree of brushing and grooming to stay healthy and neat.

>> **Broken:** Broken-coat dogs look like a blend of the other two.

© Ron Kimball Photography, Inc.

FIGURE 2-3: Two JRTs, smooth and rough.

Whether rough or broken, the coat must not be woolly. Both broken-coat and rough-coat dogs have longer hair on the jaw, creating a fuzzy-faced appearance.

TIP

Groom your dog regularly. All Jack Russell coat types shed. The more brushing you do, the less likely your dog's hair will wind up sprinkled on your clothes and carpet and in your family car.

Chapter **3**

A Day in the Life of a JRT

A Jack Russell doesn't have a long list of what he wants from you, but he does have needs: room to exercise, time with you, and patient training. This chapter fills you in on the details.

WARNING

If you live in a small apartment, don't spend much time at home, and/or are stressed by work or other factors, now is not the time for you to adopt a JRT.

Finding Room to Roam

JRTs don't need acres and acres to roam just to be happy, but the more controlled a space you can offer your Jack Russell, the easier time you'll have controlling his energy level and, as a result, his zippy nature and potentially destructive behavior. Many JRTs, however, have been raised quite successfully in the city, provided their owners have the time and inclination to properly maintain an exercise schedule for their busy little friends. That, more than anything, is the key to success in managing these little terrorists.

TWO JRTs DOUBLE THE FUN

TIP

Consider owning more than one Jack Russell Terrier. They will entertain you — and each other — for hours. A male and a female often become better friends than two dogs of the same gender, but you will need to take special precautions during estrus unless one or both dogs are spayed or neutered.

If you have more than one puppy or dog, so much the better. My terriers often wake up, bolt out the doggy door, and spend the next 30 minutes in uninterrupted play with each other until they finally feel the urge to come back in and hang out. This takes the burden off you as an owner to amuse your furry little friends and gives them both the exercise they desperately need and the companionship they desire. Having two puppies also allows them to check out perceived threats, such as an encroaching cat, without bothering you. Trust me, they will demand much of your attention through their regular activities. Any break you can give yourself by providing alternate forms of amusement will be greatly appreciated.

You also need to consider the climate in your area. People who live in temperate climates such as Southern California have an easier time accommodating their JRTs with outside exercise than people living through tough New York winters. That's not to say it can't be done, however. Remember that JRTs came from England, and the winters there aren't exactly balmy. It just means you have to do some adapting. You need to provide your JRT with a sweater and possibly paw protectors for cold, winter walks, and you need to find a suitable indoor energy outlet for your terrier when the weather prohibits an outdoor excursion.

JRTs can romp in the snow, provided they have enough protection to keep their body heat up. You have to keep an eye on them, however, to make sure they don't become overly chilled. One puppy from our very first litter was flown to a family in Alaska and has adapted quite well to her new arctic home. The vet gave the family a few tips to prevent her from getting too cold and some warning signs to watch. She's been happy and healthy ever since.

Appreciating a fenced yard

The best scenario is a house with some type of enclosed yard for your puppy or dog. This gives him some room to run, jump, and play in a controlled environment without harming himself or threatening your sanity. If at all possible, install a doggy door linking the inside of your house to your fenced yard. This arrangement gives your dog access to both your company and the great outdoors. He can decide whether to head outside to play or sun himself or to stay indoors to be with you. You will find that, if you provide an outdoor access and a few toys, your JRT often can amuse himself, taking some of the burden off your shoulders.

Most pet stores and many home-improvement centers offer a wide assortment of doggy doors for your convenience. These doors come in various sizes and configurations to match your terrier's height and weight and to fit into virtually any door, including sliding glass doors. Check out all your options before deciding that adding a doggy door is impossible.

Although many trainers disagree, I believe that potty training is made easier by this arrangement. By teaching your terrier to go outside on his own when he has to eliminate, you won't constantly have to be on the lookout for "tinkle signs." This also provides your JRT with instant relief when he decides that he has to go. Because he doesn't have to rely on you, he's more likely to head outside and prevent an accident, making your life and training easier. (Many trainers, however, believe that installing a doggy door for a puppy can make for sloppy house-training: The dog doesn't have to learn to "hold it," and the owner doesn't pay attention to the dog's schedule and needs.)

Making play dates

If the doggy door arrangement isn't possible, regular play trips are imperative to keep your JRT's energy level under control. These can be simple jaunts around the block, trips to a nearby park, or escapades all the way to a beach or a field to really burn off energy. All you need is your terrier, a little time, and a Frisbee or a ball, and you have the makings of a play date with your happy pooch! If you need more ideas about how to creatively exercise your JRT, check out Chapter 12.

Most behavior problems stem from a lack of exercise and stimulation. If you have a quiet neighborhood with plenty of back streets, your dog will be happy just seeing the sights and enjoying your company while also burning off energy. Even if you only have a few minutes and can't take the time for a walk, go outside and play with your dog for even just 10 or 15 minutes. This goes a long way toward satisfying your dog's need for companionship.

You also can use a hallway in your home to get a few minutes of wonderful exercise. You can just play fetch for ten minutes without ever leaving the comfort of your own home. As the advertising phrase goes, just do it.

Include your Jack Russell Terrier in as many activities as possible. He's a friendly little bugger who likes to explore new places and meet new people.

Living with a JRT in the city

Even if you live in an apartment or a condo, you still can make the arrangement work, provided you're committed to making an exercise program a regular routine for your dog and your family. Taking your JRT out for a five-minute walk once a week may seem like enough to you, but it won't be enough for your active little terrier. This type of exercise program only frustrates him, leaving his appetite for adventure whetted rather than satisfied. As soon as you bring your dog home from such a walk, he'll be eager to go right back out. When that opportunity doesn't arise, he'll seek his amusements elsewhere, often turning to destructive behavior to satisfy his energetic needs.

Because urban life isn't ideal for the JRT, you need to take some special steps to make the relationship work. If you are truly committed to your terrier and to your relationship together, you can make apartment-dwelling tolerable, provided you're willing and able to take daily trips to the park to let your Jack Russell stretch his legs and satisfy his senses. These trips can include playing ball, chasing birds, meeting new people, and just generally enjoying life. Keep in mind that you don't have to make a special trip. If you're headed out anyway, consider taking your JRT along to keep you company. It may do both of you some good.

Spending Time with Your JRT

Does your whole life have to be committed to this cuddly little beast? Of course not. But if space is limited, you must make up for it in other ways if your relationship is to be a happy one. Even when space is plentiful, however, your lifestyle may not allow you to give the time and attention necessary to satisfy your terrier.

If you work 80-hour weeks and live alone, your dog will be left to his own devices for a significant part of the day. This could lead to problems. Even if your Jack Russell has his own room to run in, don't assume he will take advantage of it. JRTs need playmates, either human or canine. If you have two dogs who get along well and who don't squabble when left alone, they usually can amuse themselves without difficulty. No amount of canine fun, however, can be substituted for your love and attention at regular intervals. Because Jack Russells are people-loving dogs, they aren't content to live solely with another dog as a companion. They need consistent, playful interaction with you, as well.

Appreciating your JRT's personality

To truly enjoy your JRT, spend time getting to know him and enjoying his unique personality quirks. All Jack Russell Terriers are distinctly unique, yet frighteningly similar. They all have odd behaviors that seem to permeate the breed (see Chapter 1), yet the way these behaviors manifest themselves and the way your terrier incorporates them into his own personality make him special indeed.

No one can spend time around a Jack Russell without being thoroughly entertained by his antics and amazed by his intelligence and problem-solving capabilities. You must spend time with your dog, however, to see this very charming side of his personality (see Figure 3-1). It takes commitment on your part to truly make your JRT part of the family rather than just another addition to your living room or yard. Given the chance, your Jack Russell Terrier will gladly assume the role of the family jester and will delight at doing funny things to make you laugh.

FIGURE 3-1:
Your Jack Russell Terrier needs you more than anything else.

© Ron Kimball Photography, Inc.

Spending time with your Jack Russell need not take an act of Congress or days of planning. Fifteen to 30 minutes each day is usually enough to satisfy your furry friend, provided he has ample opportunity to play on his own to relieve any additional pent-up boredom or energy he builds up during the day. He enjoys the interaction the two of you have, regardless of the activity.

REMEMBER

You'll likely tire of your JRT's favorite game long before he does, so don't feel like you have to be creative or innovative to satisfy your dog. Grab his favorite ball and head outside for a quick game of fetch or reach for the nearest sock toy for a bout of tug-of-war. This goes miles toward keeping your dog sane and healthy. Afterward, he's likely to curl up next to your feet for at least a few minutes before grabbing another toy and trying to entice you into another round of play.

Keep lots of chew toys around your JRT puppy — especially chew toys, balls and other bouncy toys, and cubes that dispense bits of food when rolled around — so that he can play on his own when you're not able to be with him. Be sure the toys are made for your puppy's strong jaws. Otherwise, he could ingest dangerous rubber pieces.

Including your JRT in everyday events

Simple daily routines can provide an opportunity to spend time with your terrier. A hike to the mailbox accompanied by your Jack Russell or a walk to visit your neighbor may be the perfect solution for accomplishing two goals in one fell swoop. But be honest with yourself. If you know in your heart that finding even this much spare time in your busy life will be a chore, you should opt for another breed (or perhaps you should set up an aquarium, instead).

You can't spend hours with your dog on the weekends and absolutely no time with him during the week and still expect your dog to be well mannered and adjusted. He simply has too much energy stored up to be satisfied with this arrangement. Smaller, more manageable time chunks work better for your Jack Russell, if not for you. Remember, time spent is not cumulative to a JRT. He needs some interaction time every day to be truly happy. Honestly evaluate your available time to see whether a JRT is right for you.

Don't leave your puppy alone for extended periods of time, especially in the house, unless you want to return to a demolition derby. Being alone is stressful to your dog.

Understanding the Importance of Patience

When your new JRT comes to live with you, his entire world has been turned upside down. He has gone from the safety and security of his litter and parents (assuming you're bringing home a puppy), and the only home he has known for the past eight weeks of his life. Suddenly, not one single thing remains the same. He has a new home, new owners, and no littermates to console him.

Imagine being thrust into a new country where you don't speak the language and know absolutely no one. It would be terrifying, to say the least! Your puppy feels much the same way. Be sensitive to your puppy's plight. Your puppy will inadvertently frustrate you, do things that make you crazy, and wake you up in the middle of the night, but keep in mind that your puppy isn't doing these things to torment you. He's scared and alone, and doing his best to adapt to his new situation.

Be as empathetic as you can during the first few weeks (and long after, truth be told) of your puppy's training. Every time you find yourself getting short-tempered, put yourself in the puppy's place and think how frustrated he must be. If you do this consistently, you may find yourself approaching things with a different point of view.

TIP

In addition, try the following two tips:

>> Make a point to spend at least a half hour each day cuddling or playing exclusively with your puppy. He'll feel more welcome in your home and will get to know you quicker.

>> Be consistent with your pup, especially in the first few weeks. Your JRT to must know understand the ground rules, and that's impossible if you keep changing them on him. Pick a few rules (like no going potty in the house) that are crucial for you to teach immediately, and train these things exactly the same way every time. If you say "No" today, it must mean "No" in two hours and in two days. It can't ever mean "Maybe."

Only by being patient will your puppy grow into a confident doggy teen. Then everyone can remark on how charming your four-legged child is!

It's All in the Details: Tips for Making a Perfect Match

Perhaps you've decided on a Jack Russell Terrier, but you still need to make some hard decisions, like whether to get a puppy or an adult dog and how to find the perfect JRT for you regardless of whether your dog is young or grown.

This part guides you through selecting your JRT, helps you evaluate your individual house and lifestyle to make absolutely sure you're willing and able to provide for this breed, and discusses whether kids and JRTs can share the same house. Jack Russell Terriers require a unique combination of space and exercise to be happy and content little dogs. You need to do some serious thinking to determine whether you and your family are prepared to provide this type of environment.

If you're still unsure whether you're really sold on this breed, read this part before making your decision. It's not easy being owned by a JRT, but it sure is fun!

Chapter **4**

Knowing What You Want in a JRT

I f you've decided you're ready to take the Jack Russell Terrier plunge, you need to decide which type of dog will best suit you and your family. Although a bouncing puppy is undeniably adorable, will she be the best match for your individual situation? Do you have very young children in your home who could be intimidated by the lightning speed and boundless energy that Jack Russell puppies characteristically exhibit? Do you have the available time to spend teaching a puppy basic house rules? Or would an adult dog be easier to handle?

All these questions and many more should be answered before you go looking for a JRT. Until you have a clear picture in your mind of what you want, you may have trouble finding just the right dog. It's like going on a road trip to an unknown destination with no map.

REMEMBER

Jack Russell Terriers aren't for everyone. Should you decide that you can't meet the demanding needs of this feisty little terrier, you haven't failed as a pet owner. It simply means that this particular breed of dog isn't right for you. Look for a lower-maintenance breed that will better suit your lifestyle.

WARNING

If you have any doubts at all, please wait to purchase a JRT. I can't stress enough that this breed isn't right for everyone.

Knowing Whether You Want a Pet or a Show Piece

Right off the bat, you need to determine whether you're interested in a show dog or a family pet. Your criteria will be very different depending on your answer. Conscientious breeders produce dogs who most closely fit their idea of the ideal Jack Russell Terrier. But is this ideal the same as yours? Although a particular breeder may have his eye on the next national title, you may be looking for a loyal pal and an amusing pet. It's important to decide whether you eventually want to breed your dog (see Chapter 10) or if you're looking for a pet who will fit in with your household and your family.

Selecting a show dog

If you're looking for a dog who eventually will be used for breeding, pay close attention to the structure, size, coat condition, health records, and conformation requirements for the breed organization you're interested in (see Chapter 2), and buy the dog who most closely fits that ideal (like the one in Figure 4-1). Your dog must be able to stand up to the rigorous testing of both the registering organization and the show-ring judges, so you should take special care to seek out and select the most perfect conformational specimen that's available and within your budget. Chances are, you need to go to a well-known breeder to find this terrier, and you will undoubtedly pay a premium for your selected show dog and pet.

REMEMBER

Consider which breed affiliation you want to be involved in because their standards for what is correct can be quite different. Both the American Kennel Club (AKC) and the Jack Russell Terrier Club of America (JRTCA) are discussed extensively in Chapters 2 and 16, and you want to be well informed as to their requirements and preferences before purchasing a puppy. You then should purchase your puppy based on that registry's requirements.

The paperwork you receive under each registry will be different, as well. If you're purchasing an AKC-registered dog for future breeding, secure the dog's papers and pedigree prior to taking your puppy home. If you're purchasing a puppy or dog under JRTCA standards, you must obtain from the breeder a Certificate of Registration if the dog is one year or older, or you can submit a five-generation pedigree and an original stud certificate with the registration application after the dog reaches one year of age. If you go the latter route, check the dog's pedigree carefully before you purchase to make sure the dog is not closely inbred (see Chapter 16 for information about pedigree). The dog will not be accepted for registry if close inbreeding is present in the pedigree.

FIGURE 4-1:
Select a Jack
Terrier who best
fits the breed
standard of the
organization with
which you plan to
register.

TIP

Bring the guidelines for the registry under which you'll be working when you go to look for your dog or puppy. This way, you can refer to those standards as you examine the puppy, paying attention to each and every conformational requirement. Remember, if you're going to breed or show in accredited competitions, this dog must match the ideal as closely as possible. Don't allow yourself to be swayed away from "perfect" by a cute face or great markings. These aren't a strong foundation for a breeding program. Although straight legs, strong hindquarters, and a correct bite may not be enough to win the hearts of friends and relatives, they go a long way toward producing sound, functional, and correct puppies.

Choosing the perfect pet

If showing isn't in your blood and you have no major maternal urges to produce litter after litter of spotted bundles, a pet-quality dog should be your goal. Please note that in no way should a pet-quality JRT be looked upon as inferior. They simply have physical characteristics that would make them less appealing for breeding or showing. These characteristics may include too much coat color, ears that are large or that don't set properly, or legs that are a little short. None of these characteristics should affect the dog's desirability as a pet.

In your quest for the ideal JRT, you may find a puppy with the perfect personality for your family but who possesses some of these physical "flaws." Don't hesitate to purchase this dog even though she doesn't fit the breed standard as ideal. Chances are, you'll be buying a fabulous friend who will go to the ends of the earth to please you. You'll soon see these physical differences as charming and unique rather than as flawed.

If you're looking to add a pet to your family rather than a show piece, pay very close attention to the personality of the dog you're considering. Is she aggressive? Or is she content to sit back and let the other dogs go first? Do you like her markings? Is she a good size for your family and your surroundings? Is she boisterous and rambunctious or pleasantly friendly? Most important, which of the available dogs appeals to you the most, for whatever reason?

REMEMBER

Sometimes you are simply drawn to a particular dog but are at a loss to explain why. That's perfectly normal! Spend a little more time with this dog to see whether you still like her. Then spend some time with the other dogs you can choose from to see whether you're still drawn back to the first dog. Trust your instincts. You know what you like, and you know what you don't like. Don't let someone talk you into a dog or a puppy whom you feel just isn't right for you.

TIP

Let yourself be led by your emotions. This is a dog you will have for a long time, so you must be comfortable with her right from the beginning. Being owned by a JRT for life is challenging enough; you should at least really like the dog who owns you.

REMEMBER

What may be right for the breeder's personality or that of an interested friend may not be right for you or your family. Every family's makeup is unique and distinct, just as every terrier has her own personality. Don't let anyone talk you out of a dog you feel is perfect unless they have a strong reason, such as a noticeable structural problem, why you shouldn't buy that particular puppy.

This is a pet with whom you'll share many years of your life — make your decision in much the same way you would choose your best friend. First and foremost you must enjoy each other, and you should be able to get along with each other for long periods at a time. A dog's personality rarely changes dramatically after she reaches eight or nine weeks of age: What you see is what you get. Keep this in mind when making your choice.

Deciding between Youth and Wisdom

At some point, you have to decide whether a puppy or an adult dog better fits your lifestyle.

When making your decision, make sure to consider your individual housing limitations. If you live in a home with a large backyard and have the room and ability to make a dog run — or at least a yard that's adequately fenced — you should be able to consider a dog or a puppy without too much concern. If, however, you're living in an apartment and you have to time your puppy's potty breaks to when you're available to take her out, and if you have limited space to devote to a puppy play area, an older puppy or dog is a better bet.

Looking at the pros and cons of puppies

A cute puppy is hard to resist. When you bring a puppy into your home, you get the opportunity to train her to be the companion you want, and you don't have to "undo" any bad habits an older dog may have developed. Although a puppy certainly will get more attention from your friends and neighbors, honestly evaluate whether you have the time and the facilities to effectively manage life with a puppy. Puppies can't be left alone to amuse themselves during the day, or you're likely to come home to a house that has been significantly redecorated! Likewise, your house-training will go smoothly only if you have the patience, time, and consistency to produce results.

Keep your living arrangements in mind, as well. If you live very close to the house next to you, a whining or barking puppy in the middle of the night will not endear you to your neighbors. Remember that any puppy will experience a period of adjustment, and some need a longer time than others. Even when the dog is grown, she still will bark at passing cars and at loud noises. If yours is the only dog on the street, you may want to consider an older dog from the start to break the neighborhood in, so to speak. If you start out with a puppy and have problems, you're likely to find an angry neighbor on your doorstep when you return home from work one day.

In addition, young children may be more comfortable with a more mature addition to the household. Not only will an older dog be a bit more forgiving of a child's exuberance, she also will be less likely to knock down a small child out of excitement and her moods will be more easily controlled. In addition, you won't have to worry about your young child accidentally stumbling upon one of your puppy's mistakes, creating a messy situation for everyone.

Evaluating the pros and cons of adult dogs

Adult dogs can be a good choice, especially if they have been spayed or neutered. They already have gone through their terrible teens and are more likely to fit into a subdued lifestyle with a minimum of fuss. They are also more likely to amicably "duke it out" with a dog who is already part of the family without becoming panicked or intimidated. Remember that you want your new addition to be a joy, not a hassle. Sometimes this means choosing a dog who is either fully or partially grown and who already has some of the basics in place for you to build on.

UNDERSTANDING THE NEED FOR PLAYMATES

Unless your Jack Russell has another dog as a companion who has an energy capacity similar her own, you can bet your dog has spent a little time playing and a lot of time sleeping. She'll be revved up and ready to go after a long, relaxing nap, so your dog isn't being bad by wanting your attention. She simply needs your company after a long day of solitude. If you ignore your dog, she's likely to drive you crazy trying to get your attention. You'll be in a much better position and frame of mind if you resolve yourself to spending some time playing with your dog when you get home from work or after a long day away from home. You then can unwind in peace, and your JRT will know that she has been acknowledged.

ANTICIPATING THE JRT REMODEL

Keep in mind that JRTs have boundless energy. If they aren't given plenty of exercise, they create their own diversions, usually the destruction of something important to you. A young puppy with no supervision and no outlet for her energy will be an unhappy puppy. Apartment training is best reserved for older dogs or for dogs with someone home most of the day who is willing to commit to a regular exercise regime. All JRTs, young and old, need plenty of companionship and exercise. If your circumstances don't currently allow for this, you may want to consider postponing your purchase of a JRT until your living conditions change.

Aside from boundless energy, Jack Russell Terriers are naturally curious by nature, always wanting to explore their surroundings and constantly on the lookout for new games with which to amuse themselves. If they aren't allowed to go outside for these diversions, each and every nook and cranny in your home becomes fair game for the industrious little terriers. Some JRTs become so destructive that they have to be crated when left at home alone. Others can be trusted (to some extent), provided they receive lots of playtime when their owner is home. The smaller the space to roam, the more likely you'll have a destruction problem.

I was told by one terrier owner about a time when he inadvertently locked his dog inside his den prior to leaving home. When he returned, the terrier had not only chewed holes in the arms of the couch, she had literally pulled the phone lines out of the walls and the carpet off the floor! Although the owner was not amused, the JRT was proud of her redecorating job and was eager for the next time she would be left in the den. It only takes one such experience to learn the lesson. These little dogs take to destruction with the same obsession they take to playing ball. They can do serious damage to a house and its furnishings in a remarkably short amount of time.

Be a bit forgiving of an older dog's mistakes in the house, at least until the ground rules are set (see Chapter 8). Her previous owners may have had different boundaries than you do, and your dog needs a period of adjustment to understand what is expected of her in her new home.

Keep in mind, however, that a more mature dog may be a bit more set in her ways. If her previous handling has been good, this shouldn't be a problem. But if her previous owners had trouble with training, you may be inheriting someone else's problems. In this case, an older puppy — say six or seven months old — may be a good compromise. JRTs that age are still are young enough to accept change but are old enough to control themselves and to understand right from beginning what the ground rules should be.

Considering Jack Russell rescue

Rescuing a JRT who has fallen on hard times may be an option to consider when adopting your terrier. It's a wonderful feeling to know that, not only are you adding to your family, you're also helping save a life that wouldn't have such a rosy future if no suitable home were found for her. Just because a dog is coming from the rescue doesn't mean she's defective or inferior in any way. Most of these dogs simply have ended up in situations where they were misunderstood or abandoned.

Some dogs end up in rescue facilities because their owners develop financial problems or have to make a change in their living arrangements that prevents them from taking along their dog. Some dogs are given up by people who, unlike you, didn't do their research before purchasing a dog and ended up with more than they bargained for. Many of these dogs can be adopted and readily taken into families, provided the new family is willing and able to properly care for them.

REMEMBER

JRT is not the breed for everyone. In reality, few people and families are dedicated to this type of "special needs" pet. If not handled properly, their destructive nature can drive away even the most understanding owner, and their odd behaviors can scare off even the most grounded personality. A sense of humor is an important trait in a Jack Russell owner, as is a solid savings account for unexpected home repairs.

Even though the warnings are repeated relentlessly to new JRT owners, few truly understand what "high energy" means until they have brought home their bundle of joy. Few have experienced the frustrations of trying to bend a terrier's personality to their own will. It complicates matters even more when you consider the extreme intelligence of these sturdy little dogs, because no owner likes to be outsmarted by their dog! The prior owners of the rescue terriers didn't necessarily fail, they simply underestimated the personality of the JRT and overestimated their abilities to manage the dog.

One benefit of adopting a rescue dog is that they usually are spayed or neutered prior to placement, relieving you of that financial burden. Also, most of rescue dogs have received some professional handling during their temporary rescue placement. This enables you to get accurate feedback about the dog's personality and quirks. All prospective homes are screened to make sure the terrier doesn't end up in a bad situation again. This is why it is important to consider all the factors involved and to make an educated decision whether this breed is right for you prior to committing to a dog.

The handlers at Russell Rescue are apt to ask you a long list of questions to determine whether you're truly serious in your commitment to a JRT. They want to know whether you understand the requirements of the breed and are prepared to handle the energy level, personality quirks, and sometimes-aggressive tendencies in the dog. They will inquire about your living arrangements and the facilities available for the dog. They may ask whether you have children and, if so, what their ages are.

These questions aren't meant to be intrusive; the rescue staff simply is trying to make sure the terrier is going to someone fully educated about the benefits and drawbacks of the breed and someone who has a home that satisfies the spatial requirements of the dog (see Chapter 3). It's the staff's job to make sure the rescued JRT doesn't end up in a poorly prepared home or with an unsuspecting family. They take their jobs quite seriously. All who have worked with this breed have a true affinity for these dogs and feel quite protective of their futures. They're simply trying to find the best home for each dog's unique needs, and they want to make sure the potential owners are fully educated and ready to accept the terrier challenge.

REMEMBER

Keep in mind that you may not want to get involved with some rescue cases. Some of these dogs have been abused prior to placement at the rescue, and some need special emotional and physical care as a result of their misfortune. Caring for a healthy, unabused JRT is one thing, but caring for a dog with a significant negative history is quite another. I would venture to say that few first-time terrier owners truly can understand the magnitude of this challenge. Many of the quirks and traits of JRTs are magnified in an abused dog, truly creating a Jack Russell terror. If you're not totally committed to providing for the special physical and emotional needs of many rescue dogs, pass on that particular dog, especially if this is your first terrier.

Most of the time, the rescue JRT's only sin was acting like a terrier with owners who were unprepared for this behavior. (Many people see the charming little dog on the television screen and have fantasies of owning the perfect dog just like Wishbone. Although they certainly are charming, Jack Russells are far from perfect, and they often can be frustrating. Remember that years of training have gone into making these perfect little screen actors.) Even after ten years, a terrier will still be a terrier. A JRT will never have the same personality as a Labrador Retriever or a St. Bernard.

Chapter **5**

Finding Your Soulmate

Without question, the best place to get a puppy is from a reputable breeder's establishment. Good breeders work to produce healthy, well-adjusted dogs, and they're honest in their representations of their dogs' assets and less-desirable qualities. A good breeder is fully aware of the Jack Russell's needs and quirks and can be very helpful in working with you to select the right puppy for you. In fact, a reputable breeder will try to dissuade you from buying a puppy from him if he feels that none of his particular pups fits into your lifestyle or if he feels that a Jack Russell simply isn't a good match for you and your family.

REMEMBER

The Jack Russell isn't for everyone and requires a special family for both parties to be happy. When you purchase a puppy from a concerned breeder, you'll be provided with breed-specific information, information about the puppy's parents, and information about his upbringing. You'll also receive records of the puppy's vaccinations and the documentation necessary to register your dog with any of the registries, unless the dog already comes with AKC accreditation.

TIP

As a prospective JRT owner, spend a lot of time shopping for your future pet and be prepared to ask lots of questions. Not only can you take advantage of the vast knowledge that breeders have about JRTs, you can also determine which breeder and which specific puppy will be right for your family.

Rather than risk the chance of purchasing an unhealthy puppy or a puppy who can't be registered in the future if you so desire, seek out a known JRT breeder in your area and view the puppies available for purchase. These breeders can be found through the classifieds in the newspaper, through local pet stores, or even through a veterinarian's office. If you don't have any luck with these sources, contact the AKC and the JRTCA directly (see Chapters 16 and 18) to ask for the names of breeders in your area. Keep in mind that prices and types of dogs vary widely from breeder to breeder and from location to location.

Understanding That Cost Is Only One Factor

When looking through ads and talking to breeders, keep in mind that the cheapest puppy isn't always your best buy, and your choice shouldn't be based on price alone. If possible, make price your least important factor (within reason, of course) to avoid making a mistake. Focus instead on the puppy's personality, temperament, markings, and breeding to make your decision. Finding a puppy within your budget is important, but try to be a little flexible to get the right terrier for your family.

Reviewing the Take-Back Policy

As important as it is to find the right puppy, it is equally important for you to be comfortable with the breeder you select. Not all breeders are created equal, and their policies on litters can vary widely. Most reputable breeders have a take-back policy on all their puppies. This means that if, at any time, for whatever reason, the puppy doesn't work out for you or your family, the breeder will take back the puppy and place it in another home. You also have the option to try to sell the puppy on your own first, but a take-back policy is a good option if you don't have time to sell the puppy yourself or if your efforts have failed. Although you lose the money you paid for the dog, you don't have to put it in an animal shelter or place it with Russell Rescue (see Chapters 4 and 16). You can be fairly sure the puppy will be placed in a loving home.

Most breeders are genuinely concerned about their puppies and want to find the best homes for them. They'd rather take the puppy back and go through the process of finding him another home than see the dog go to a home in which his future would be questionable. No breeder likes to see one of his terriers end up in

Russell Rescue. A take-back policy proves that the breeder is concerned about both the short- and long-term welfare of the puppies she produces and that she's not just out to make a quick buck.

Ask breeders for references from previous puppy buyers. Most breeders will be happy to give you this information because they're proud of their dogs and their successes. If the breeder is reluctant to provide references, look elsewhere.

Asking Questions

Just as you're evaluating the puppies presented to you, evaluate the honesty of the breeder doing the presenting.

Most breeders are happy to talk about the puppies they've produced, the homes in which they were placed, and almost anything and everything to do with their dogs. Sometimes they talk too much about their dogs! However irritating this may be, it's a good sign. It shows that they're educated about their dogs and are willing to share that knowledge with you, the new owner.

Using your breeder as a resource

Breeders who are reluctant to share information and stories about their dogs either are hiding something in their backgrounds or are out of touch with their dogs and the dogs' personalities. Either way, you're not likely to get the solid information you need to make your decision. The breeder is the best source available for determining which puppy has which personality. After talking with you and your family, the breeder should be able to point you in the right direction toward a particular pup.

From birth, puppies — like people — have distinct and individual personalities. Some are more playful, some are more reserved, some are more aggressive, and some are more timid. These traits are unlikely to change much as the puppy grows into adulthood and are a good indicator as to whether the dog will fit in with your family and your lifestyle.

Most breeders can easily give you details about his puppies' personalities, and it is important for you to ask him straight out which puppy fits the requirements you're looking for. If he suggests a puppy you're not naturally drawn to, ask him why he feels this puppy is right for you. He may have very good reasons for his choice, and you probably do well to keep an open mind. Remember that the breeder has lived with these pups for several weeks and has had the opportunity to view them in a variety of situations. He knows the puppies' personalities better than anyone else and should be able to give you concrete examples of each puppy's typical behavior.

Don't be afraid to ask a breeder about the type of person he feels the breed is best suited for. If he tells you that JRTs will fit in anywhere and that they get along with almost everyone, he clearly is out of touch with his dogs or wants to make a sale at any cost. If he tells you that terriers are eccentric, that they need tons of exercise, that they may not do well with extremely young children, and that they are likely to pick a fight with every Rottweiler on the block, you can rest assured you're probably getting some straightforward answers.

Looking at health issues

Don't forget to ask about the puppy's vaccination record, whether his *dewclaws* (nails on the back of the dog's legs) have been removed, when his next shots are due, and when his tail was docked. Most breeders will volunteer this type of information in writing, but some get so busy visiting that they forget to provide this to you. You also should ask whether the breeder provides either a Certificate of Registration from the AKC or a complete, five-generation pedigree of the puppy and a Stud Certificate for JRTCA so that you can register your puppy when he's old enough. All this paperwork should accompany the puppy when you take him home.

The breeder should also provide the name of the puppy food that the puppies have been started on and, ideally, should give you a small supply of food to get you started until you can go to the pet store to buy your own. It's important that you feed your puppy the same brand and type of food he has been eating to minimize the stomach upset and illness that can accompany the stresses of a new home and environment. If that brand is unavailable in your area, ask what the primary ingredients are in the dog food so you can match it closely with another brand. See Chapter 11 for more on nutrition.

Getting ready to get grilled

Another good sign is if the breeder asks you lots of questions, such as whether you've ever been around Jack Russell Terriers before and what type of home you have. He's not trying to be nosy; he's just concerned about whether you know what you're getting into by purchasing a JRT. Jack Russells are high-energy dogs with unique and odd personalities and clearly are not for everyone. A good breeder will be well aware of this fact and may even try to sway you away from the breed in favor of something more docile. He will want to hear that you've carefully thought your decision through and are well aware of the peculiarities of the breed. He also will want reassurance that you're aware of the exercise and environmental needs of the breed and have researched your decision thoroughly.

Choosing perfect parents

If possible, spend some time with the puppy's *sire* (father) and *dam* (mother) of the litter. The personalities of the litter's parents will give you a good idea of what the puppies' temperaments will be like. Two very aggressive dogs are likely to produce aggressive puppies, and two hyper dogs are likely to produce an extremely active litter.

REMEMBER

When evaluating the puppy's parents, keep in mind that you're a stranger to their home, and they are apt to be more active, inquisitive, and protective than usual. Give them some leeway to account for this disruption in their routine and take that into account when evaluating their personalities. Ideally, you will find two friendly and energetic dogs that will try to engage you in play or mooch for attention. They should be active without appearing out of control, and they should be likeable and approachable.

WARNING

If a parent is intimidated by your presence or seems overly hostile, it is a sign that these tendencies may run throughout the litter. You may want to pass on this group of pups.

Reaching maturity milestones

Beware of any breeder who is willing to let his puppies leave their home at younger than eight weeks of age. Some breeders make an exception of a week or so if they know the new owners extremely well and are assured they have the appropriate knowledge to care for a puppy this young. As a rule, however, the puppy should not leave before the eight-week-old mark. Prior to that time, the puppies are still learning an important lesson from their mom and each other. Waiting until the eight-week date ensures that the puppy is both physically mature and emotionally secure enough to handle the separation from both his mother and his littermates.

Picking the Perfect Puppy

Shopping for a new car, a new home, or new furniture can be overwhelming with hundreds of color, size, and design choices. The same can be said for shopping for a new JRT puppy. Not only do you have gender and coat types to decide on, you also have a huge variety of colorings, leg lengths, and personalities that makes each individual puppy unique. And they're all so cute! Just like shopping for a car, however, it's easy to be swayed away from your original goal by a cute face and smooth-talking breeder.

This is why, after careful consideration and long talks with all family members involved, it is crucial for you to record your preferences in writing before you begin puppy hunting. By committing this wish list in writing, you're less likely to take a wrong turn and end up with something different from what you really want. Have a particular type of puppy in mind and then go looking for the puppy that most closely fits your criteria.

TIP

Develop a plan and stick with it. All puppies are adorable, and you can easily get caught up in a bouncing bundle of fuzz. Remember, however, that you'll be living with this particular terrier for a very long time, even after he's old and gray.

When you're satisfied that you've found a breeder you're comfortable with and breeding stock that fits your idea of worthy parents, its time to move on to the individual puppies within the litter. Be careful about getting to this step prior to the other evaluations. You could find yourself inextricably wound up around a furry little paw and make a poor decision regardless of logic or reason!

Watching the litter interact

Look carefully at the puppies in the litter, especially those who fit your gender requirements. Does one immediately catch your eye? If so, focus more on that puppy and notice how he interacts with his littermates. Is he playful and energetic? Or is he timid or listless? Does he seem to be the attacker or the attackee (see Figure 5-1)? Does he interact with any toys or chewies in his surroundings? Or is he more interested in either the other puppies or you, the stranger? All these behaviors give you clues about the puppy's personality.

FIGURE 5-1:
These puppies
are just playing!

Checking out your choice

After you watch the puppy interact, ask to have him taken out of the kennel or to an area away from the rest of the litter. Does the puppy appear to be intimidated? Or is he happy to amuse himself with your attentions? Are you able to engage the puppy in play? Does he appear to be timid or a little feisty? Note these personality traits and compare them to the list of desired characteristics you made prior to setting out on your puppy-hunting expedition.

TIP

Take your wish list with you and have one of your family members keep it at all times. Before committing to a certain puppy, have all family members review the list and come to an agreement that you're making the right decision.

Assessing temperament

Pick up the puppy and handle him. Does the puppy wriggle and try to get away? Or does he sit quietly in your arms, perhaps trying to lick your nose? Is the puppy content to be with you? Or is he constantly trying to get back to the pack? Are you able to put the puppy on his back without a major battle? Is the puppy interested in what you're doing? Does he try to attack your finger or is he more curious about your actions?

Most puppies don't like being held upside down but will accept the position after a bit of coercion. This is a good test to see whether the puppy will tend to be assertive or timid by nature. If the puppy fights this action tooth and nail, you probably have a more aggressive puppy and one who is likely to be a bit on the feisty side. Although this isn't necessarily a bad quality, it is something you should know prior to selecting the puppy as your ideal pet. This is a dog who will take a firmer hand in training and is likely to be a bit more strong-willed when growing up. He also is one who will defend you ferociously, however, if he feels you're being threatened.

REMEMBER

Think about the type of dog you set out to find. If you're looking for a quiet dog who will curl up at your feet each night and socialize well with other dogs and people, you may want to look for a puppy who exhibits a more laid-back behavior, at least by JRT standards. If you're looking for a dog to go hunting with you or to wrestle with you and your buddies, a more assertive puppy would be the perfect match.

Remember that when I refer to a quiet JRT, I'm not referring to a Labrador or a Great Dane. Terriers are terriers, and there is no such thing as a truly docile JRT. The Jack Russell was bred to have boundless energy and remarkable stamina, and they live up to their heritage quite nicely. Although these qualities are great for people with an active lifestyle, they aren't so hot if you and your family would rather snuggle by the fire and read a book. Of course, Jack Russells will wind down after a long day, but they never will be described as mellow dogs.

WARNING

Don't choose a puppy based strictly on emotion. Try to evaluate your desires and to include everyone in the family decision. If it doesn't feel just right, pass on the puppy until you find one that does. This is a big commitment!

Aiming for the center

In general, it is good to pick a puppy who is active and friendly but who is not the leader of the pack. If you choose a puppy who falls on either end of the scale — one who is very timid or very aggressive — you need to accept that this puppy will take special handling and training to fit into your lifestyle. Be forewarned that an overly timid puppy may become a dog who is so intimidated that he lashes out by biting. This is especially important to avoid if you have young children because they often will unintentionally overwhelm a more timid dog. Likewise, an aggressive puppy could grow into a dog who inadvertently knocks down a child or who "plays" with children by grabbing their pant legs and shaking his head. This could cause your child to take an unnecessary tumble.

Don't assume you'll be able to change the puppy as he grows. Rarely is an owner able to effectively change the basic personality of a dog. An active or assertive puppy is likely to stay that way as he matures, and a puppy who is fearful may well be a danger as an adult — withdrawing one minute and snapping the next. Instead of trying to buy a puppy and mold him into your perfect terrier, it is to your benefit to choose a dog with a personality you like. You still need to train your dog, but the training will be more successful.

No one can change the world, and trying to change a terrier's personality can be frustrating at best, futile at worst. Know what you want and pick the puppy who best fits that description.

Taking a family poll

Remember to ask the opinion of all family members before deciding on one particular puppy. What may be perfect to you may rub your partner the wrong way. And what may be great for the two of you may be totally wrong for your child. All these factors are important and should be weighed equally before a decision is made.

Determining whether looks matter

If you intend to show or breed your dog (see Chapter 4), be very selective about the puppy's adherence to the breed standard (flip to Chapter 2). If this is important to you, it must be high on your list of requirements, and you may have to pass on a particularly charming dog who just isn't show quality.

Don't pick a puppy with the idea of changing his personality. (It didn't work with your spouse, did it?) It will be less frustrating for both of you to choose a dog who naturally fits in with your family.

One last thing to remember is that both the JRTCA and the AKC lean toward the medium- to longer-legged dogs for their registered stock. Although the short-legged dogs certainly are charming, they are frowned upon by the majority of the registries. If you want to register your dog, choose a pup from taller parents whose offspring fit the guidelines for the breed and steer clear of the short-legged dogs or check out registration possibilities with the English Jack Russell Terrier Club of America (EJRTCA). If registration isn't important, enjoy the variety available to you in picking out your perfect pooch!

TIP

BUYING FROM PET STORES

Buying your puppy from a reputable breeder is always your best bet for a quality terrier. But what happens if you absolutely fall in love with that face in the pet store window and just can't get beyond those huge brown eyes? Here are some suggestions on how to make sure your fantasy doesn't turn to heartache and lots of vet bills down the road.

- **Establish some background on the puppy.** Keep in mind that many pet stores won't have the kind of detailed information and pedigrees that are available from a breeder. The pet store should be able, however, to provide you with a medical history, including shots and wormings that have been done; infomation on whether the puppy can be registered and, if so, with which registry; age of the puppy; and a list of medical problems, if any. The pet store probably won't be able to provide much in the way of a personality profile, so you'll have to try to determine whether the puppy's demeanor suits your family.

- **Give the puppy a good inspection.** Look at the puppy to be sure that his eyes are bright, there are no signs of fleas or other insects on the puppy, his skin is pink and healthy, and he shows no raw or hot spots on his back or legs. The puppy's gums should be pink and his teeth free from any buildup. He should appear energetic and inquisitive without being sluggish or overly aggressive. If the pup strikes you as being quite calm or lackluster, I suggest passing on this puppy, even if you have your heart set on him.

- **Ask what kind of guarantee comes with the puppy.** In other words, what happens if you get your terrier home and a week later she inexplicably dies or ends up in the vet's office with medical complications? You should be able to get some remedy from the pet store if this occurs. Most reputable pet stores offer some type of guarantee as to the health of the puppies they sell. If the pet store clerks appear hedgy, I suggest going elsewhere.

Remember that your JRT will be with you for years to come, so if you have any doubts, proceed with caution!

3
Setting Out the Welcome Mat

In this part, you get advice about how to introduce your new dog or puppy to existing family members, both two-legged and four-legged. Terriers, by nature, are rather difficult little creatures, so this part helps you identify specific danger zones in and around your house and provides directions to make these places a little safer.

If you know how to terrier-proof your house and employ some simple training techniques, you can make living with your Jack Russell Terrier a little more predictable. Although you never totally control your JRT's antics, this part gives you some valuable tools for tempering your terrier's temperament.

Finally, this part discusses how to be a firm but benevolent leader for your terrier, gives some basic training guidelines that every JRT and terrier owner should know, and helps you understand the use of positive reinforcement and corrections in your training. You can also read up on how to deal with dogs who have specific problems such as barking, digging, aggression, separation anxiety, chewing, and chasing.

Chapter **6**

Dog-Proofing Your Home

Your home and your yard can be full of hazards for a young, exuberant puppy. Prevention is often the best strategy for a Jack Russell Terrier. A few steps now can save you headaches and heartaches in the future — this chapter shows you how.

And after you've dog-proofed your JRT's new home, you're ready to welcome her into your household. This chapter shares a few tips on helping your new Jack Russell get along with children and existing pets.

Puppy-Proofing 101

By providing a suitable environment for your puppy and by taking some measures to "puppy-proof" your home prior to bringing your terrier home, you can prevent many accidents that could frustrate you and be dangerous for your pet. Many times, these accidents come about because new owners simply don't look at their homes from a puppy's point of view, and they overlook obvious temptations that could prove hazardous or just too tempting for the little explorer to resist.

Like small children who learn by exploring, your JRT puppy will find every cord, string, and sock to be an amusing toy or a convenient teething target. She sees things much differently than an adult dog would and uses all her senses to explore and understand her surroundings. And like a small child, almost everything a puppy finds will soon make her way into her mouth.

As a new puppy owner, you need to understand that your JRT isn't trying to be purposefully destructive; she simply is using her mouth as an instrument to learn about her new surroundings. Because she has no hands, her mouth becomes the obvious alternative. Although a sock or favorite slipper finding her way into your puppy's mouth can do more to frustrate you than to harm your puppy, other tempting toys may injure or kill her if they end up within her reach. This is where you need to think like a JRT and locate obvious tempting trouble areas before your puppy does.

Avoiding the zap attack

Puppies love to chew on electrical cords and are often equally fascinated by their outlet cousins. Although it can be frustrating for you to unplug all of your appliances every day, the cords can be dangerous or even deadly to your Jack Russell Terrier. If the cord is plugged into the socket and your dog happens upon the live portion of the cord, your puppy could receive a serious shock resulting in burns, damaged tissue, or even death. The same can occur if your puppy licks a wall socket and the saliva comes in contact with a live connection.

To prevent this from happening, make a conscious effort to keep all loose cords from dangling within your puppy's reach and use plastic socket covers to eliminate exposed socket connections. If the cord has to run along the baseboard or along the base of a lamp or appliance, anchor the cord securely along its path to prevent it from moving about as the puppy brushes against it — a sure lure for your puppy's attention. If your puppy does sustain a shock, wrap her in a towel and call your veterinarian immediately for further instructions.

WARNING

If your dog has suffered an electric shock, disconnect the power cord before touching her. This prevents further injury to your dog and eliminates the chance that you may receive a shock while handling your pet.

Looking out for tower terrors

Puppies love to look at new and enticing things, and they aren't often picky about where those things are located. Because a puppy is small, more often than not the interesting item is above her head, and she will go to great lengths to get a closer look. Many puppies and dogs are injured every year by jumping up onto or against unstable pieces of furniture such as end tables or bookcases. If the puppy hits something with enough force, it could fall on top of her, crushing her beneath its bulk. Make sure that all furniture within the puppy's realm is base-stable and that no balls or other interesting toys are placed on objects with the potential to tip over and crush the puppy, just in case she tries to reach the item on her own.

Looking for friends in high places

Like many young children, puppies like to climb on things so they can feel on top of the world and everything in it. Depending on your individual house, this can mean climbing everything from staircases to balconies. The only problem with this particular fascination is that puppies also have short attention spans and can become fixated on an object. When this happens, the puppy easily can forget that she's several feet off the ground and will literally walk off an edge to explore something several feet away.

REMEMBER

Jack Russell Terriers are born jumpers and often can jump several feet in the air to get their favorite sock or ball. They can also misjudge a drop-off, however, and can break or sprain a leg if they jump too far.

TRY THIS

To prevent your puppy from inadvertently taking a tumble over a dangerous edge, place temporary fencing around all high, enticing places. Better yet, place a removable gate at the base of the stairs leading to these places to prevent your puppy from getting herself too high off the ground. If the balcony is outside, a temporary barrier of chicken wire or fine mesh fencing can be used to keep your puppy safe and sound. It won't exactly make an exterior design fashion statement, but it's easy to put up, is easy to remove, and is worth the peace of mind you gain with regard to your puppy's safety.

Dealing with doors

Doors are an unavoidable feature in every house, but they also can be a hidden danger for your dog or puppy. Because of a Jack Russell Terrier's size and her penchant for always following you around the house, it's easy to forget that your puppy may be at your heels. You may slam a door without even thinking about it, catching your puppy between the door and the jamb. Every year, hundreds of dogs are treated for broken legs and tails caused by just this scenario, and some suffer even worse injuries as a result of their owners' unintended actions.

To prevent this from happening, install latches on the backs of your doors to prevent a person or the wind from slamming the door shut on your puppy. This can at least minimize any damage that may occur by providing a cushion of space for the leg or the tail should the door suddenly swing shut, trapping the limb.

Keep an especially close eye on swinging doors. Not only can they pick up speed and force by swinging to and fro, the puppy can also try to ease herself through and then get her head caught as the door closes, leading to possible strangulation. Whenever a puppy is around these doors, they should be either blocked open or blocked closed to prevent inquiring minds from getting themselves in trouble.

Glass doors also pose a threat to your high-energy JRT puppy. Remember that your terrier is likely to go flying through your house at breakneck speeds, and a clear-glass door easily could look like no door at all. It's not hard to envision the damage that could ensue should your puppy decide to go flying through what she thinks is an open space. An accompanying sliding screen door or a few decals placed at doggy level can help your puppy realize that a door is coming up and should help prevent an injury of this type.

Realize, too, that any door leading outside should be carefully watched unless it leads to a secure, fenced yard. Open doors are irresistible to most JRTs, and they often are out like a flash before you even realize they were nearby. Screen doors are invaluable if you own a terrier because even the most conscientious owners have been caught unaware by their Jack Russells streaking through their legs when they least expected it. At least a screen door gives them something to bounce off of if they hit it.

If you have children or visitors in the house, make sure they are aware of the importance of keeping all exterior doors closed. Instill in your terrier a sense of respect for the words "No!" and "Stay!" so you can prevent her from dashing outside and getting into trouble.

Keeping your JRT away from garage doors

WARNING

Garage doors, especially electric ones, also can pose a threat to your terrier. The best solution is to keep your JRT out of the garage when opening or closing the door. If this isn't possible, however, catch and hold your terrier whenever closing the door. Even doors with sensors can exert enough pressure to crush your dog, so don't rely on these "safety features" to protect your puppy. A manual door that's allowed to swing closed on its own also can crush your puppy, so be sure of your terrier's whereabouts before closing any garage doors.

Protecting your Jack Russell from perilous poisons

Curious by nature, JRTs seem to have a way of finding the most dangerous substances in the most unlikely places. By being aware of common household cleaners and plants that could be toxic to your puppy, you can minimize, if not eliminate, the threat of accidental poisoning.

Plants that are no-no's in the JRT abode include the following:

- Azaleas
- Castor bean
- Corn cockle
- English holly berries
- Foxglove
- Jimson weed
- Milkweed
- Mistletoe
- Oleander
- Philodendron and its rhododendron cousins
- Rattlebox
- Water hemlock

Check with local nurseries to find out about other plants indigenous to your area that may pose a threat to your puppy.

Cleaners and common household utensils also can be life-threatening to your dog, and you may not even realize they pose a threat until its too late. Keep the following away from your puppy:

- Insect and rodent baits
- Household cleaners
- Paint thinner
- Gasoline and antifreeze
- Prescription and over-the-counter drugs
- Toilet cleaners and air fresheners
- Laundry and dish detergents
- Insecticides, plant foods, and some fertilizers

Many of these substances have a sweet smell or taste that can be enticing to dogs.

Even such common items as nuts, bolts, loose change, and beads can pose a choking hazard to your puppy, and sharp objects such as pins and needles can wreak havoc on your dog's internal organs. If you don't want your children getting into something, it's probably equally unsafe for your puppy. Keep all such items out of the sight and reach of your terrier.

HAPPY, HEALTHY HOLIDAYS

The holidays can present their own temptations and troubles for your Jack Russell Terrier. Even older dogs can get lured into trouble by the brightly colored baubles and enticingly wrapped packages. As with the furniture, a Christmas tree easily can crush a puppy if it falls. If at all possible, the two should never be in the same room together. Likewise, a puppy may mistake the scent of the tree for the scent of the great outdoors, and your packages could end up with a decidedly doggy touch. Try explaining that to friends and family! But always remember that your puppy isn't intentionally misbehaving. She's simply getting confused by the decorations and temptations and is acting as any youngster would do — with curiosity.

Packages and their wrappings can be too tempting for your puppy to ignore and could result in a toxic reaction or strangulation if you're not careful. A balled-up piece of wrapping paper may look like trash to you, but it looks like a fun toy to your puppy. Some of today's wrapping papers contain dyes and foils that can wreak havoc on your puppy's digestive tract. If she swallows a piece, it may lead to a toxic reaction.

Likewise, long ribbons are fun to roll around with, but they easily can get wrapped around your puppy's neck and cause strangulation. When you're opening presents, put your puppy in another room or in an area where she can't get to the presents and wrappings.

Holiday foods and trimmings also can pose a threat to your puppy or dog. Foods such as chocolate, turkey, and chicken bones (or any bones small enough to be swallowed) and holiday decorations such as mistletoe and poinsettias can be deadly if ingested by your Jack Russell Terrier. Make sure that neither you nor your guests, even with the best of intentions, share the holiday meal with your dog. You also need to keep all dangerous plants and decorations out of your terrier's reach. If you want to be generous, buy your puppy a present of her own, such as a new chew toy.

Call your vet if your dog has convulsions, is vomiting, is staggering, or has collapsed. All can be signs of poisoning and should be attended to immediately. Also call the vet if you notice that your terrier's breathing has become labored, extremely rapid, shallow, loud, or irregular, or if she gasps for breath, displays a blue tongue, or loses consciousness. Any of these symptoms can indicate that your dog is choking.

Taking a Look at Outdoor Safety Tips

In addition to removing any toxic plants from your yard that could be dangerous to your puppy, you also must make your puppy's fencing truly terrier-proof. Sometimes small holes or weaknesses in the fence go unnoticed by you but act like magnets to your would-be roamer. If she finds one of these weaknesses, she will be sure to capitalize on her good fortune.

Terriers of all types are known to be diggers, and a yard that seems dig-proof to you may be easily circumvented by your crafty canine. All fences surrounding your puppy's play area should extend below the ground's surface and should be at least five feet tall. If the fence already is in place and can't be changed, add a sturdy mesh barrier below the fence that extends at least 8 to 12 inches underground to keep your digging demon safely at home. Eyeball the span of the fence to make sure there are no obvious holes or weak spots that your terrier can take advantage of.

If you must leave your puppy or dog alone in the backyard, check that all gates are securely closed and locked both to keep your terrier inside and to keep any intruders or doggy-nappers out. Make sure all plants and trees are free from any sharp or jagged edges that could impale a jumping or running puppy, and remove any fruits or pine cones in danger of falling or are too close to the ground. If you own a pool, the surrounding fence and gate should be in good shape without any penetrable holes, and the gate must be securely shut and fastened. Even a wheelbarrow like the one in Figure 6-1 can injure your JRT if the wheelbarrow tips forward.

Leaving your JRT outside during an extended absence isn't necessarily a perfect solution. A JRT can be a persistent and innovative little creature. If you leave your terrier outside with only a screen door separating her from the inside of your cozy home, you may come home to find your terrier happily dozing on your couch with a very large hole in your screen door. Similarly, if you leave your terrier outside for long periods of time without distractions or supervision, you're likely to return home to find each and every bulb you've planted dug up and strewn across your yard or to discover a very large hole beneath the fence that separates your home from your neighbor's backyard.

FIGURE 6-1:
With JRTs, even a
wheel barrow can
be hazardous.

JRTs do well outside, provided they have plenty of food and water to satisfy them for the length of time you'll be gone, a cozy bed to sleep in, and lots of toys to amuse them (see Figure 6-2). If the space is too small to allow running off some energy, you could be setting yourself up for a persistent digging problem. Take that into consideration when you plan your run. Also remember that your terrier needs some protection from the elements. If the forecaster is predicting rain, make sure that your dog can easily go inside a doghouse or under a shelter to stay dry. If it's going to be very hot outside, make sure to provide shade as a relief from the sun.

WARNING

Always make sure to supply your dog with plenty of water while you're away. One of the leading causes of hospitalization for dogs is dehydration, so don't overlook this important detail.

Another thing to consider is that JRTs have remarkable jumping ability. Make sure the fence around your doggy run is high enough to prevent an unintended escape. With most terriers, this means a minimum of five to six feet high. It may need to be higher, however, if your terrier is particularly tenacious or athletic.

TIP

Don't relegate your puppy or dog to an enclosed corner of your yard all the time. Your dog wants and needs to be included in your family activities.

FIGURE 6-2:
Provide toys for
your backyard
Jack Russell.

© Ken and Donna Dannen/ACK Stock Images

Using Sanity Savers from the Start

TRY THIS

Before bringing your new JRT home, consider purchasing the following sanity savers:

>> **Baby gate:** If you choose to use a gate to cordon off your puppy's area, be sure to select one that's high enough to prevent your puppy from jumping or climbing over the top and that easily and firmly spans the width of the door opening. Also remember to put your puppy on a surface that can easily be cleaned, such as linoleum or cement, and to provide a soft place for your puppy to lie down, such as a blanket or a doggy bed. To prevent boredom, give your puppy a toy or chewie (or both) to amuse herself while you're gone.

>> **Doggy crate:** If you choose the crate approach (see the "It's a crate life!" section in this chapter, along with Chapters 7 and 9), remember to choose one that's the correct size, and never leave your dog or puppy crated for a long period of time. (This creates a frustrated dog that sleeps while you're away and that drives you crazy for attention while you're home.) If you must leave your dog for an extended period of time, leave her either outside in a backyard or in a large dog exercise area so her abundant energy has an outlet. Better yet, provide a companion dog to keep your terrier company.

For the short haul, a crate can be a sanity saver and actually can be comforting for your dog. Whether you choose the plastic travel crate or the wire mesh variety, your dog actually can learn to love her makeshift den. The crate is best used when housebreaking a puppy (see Chapter 7), during the night for destructive or mischievous dogs (flip to Chapter 9), or for short periods while you're away from home if your dog has a hard time controlling her destructive tendencies (also covered in Chapter 9). It can also be used as a way to separate dogs as necessary as a place for a time-out when your dog becomes overstimulated.

TIP

Make your puppy's crate or confined area a pleasant place to be by paying attention to her surroundings. It should be a quiet place that is neither too hot nor too cold, and it should have good ventilation. (Of course, always provide fresh water while you're away.)

WARNING

Don't leave your terrier in her crate or otherwise separated from you and your family when you're home as well as when you're away. Jack Russells want to be involved. They learn from interaction with you and your family during periods of freedom away from their safe enclosures.

>> **Exercise pen:** A nice way to confine your dog is to use an exercise pen that can be fitted together to provide a smaller or larger enclosure, depending on your needs. These pens have the added benefit of being portable, so you can use them when traveling with your dog or when attending terrier trials and play-days. Because they're flexible, you only need to take as many panels as you need, and they even can be made into two pens if you have more than one pet.

For a daytime kennel, exercise pens can be great for curtailing destructive behavior and for limiting housetraining mistakes. They are large enough to give your puppy room to move, but they don't encompass such a large area that your terrier is likely to get into any serious trouble. These pens can be placed inside or outside, and they don't rely on a suitable doorway or opening as a gate does. They stand alone and allow you to place them almost anywhere, adding to your confinement options. You also can use puppy pads or newspaper in one corner to minimize the mess to clean up when house-training.

As with all enclosures and crates, make sure to provide plenty of water during your absence, a soft place to take a nap, and plenty of toys and chewies for amusement. Make sure the area is free of unnecessary distractions that could rile up your puppy while you're away. Try to make the area as quiet and soothing as possible so your puppy will learn to relax when placed in this area. Soon your puppy will learn to enjoy her own little domain!

Introducing Your JRT to Her New Home

Now that you have fully dog-proofed your home, you're ready to introduce that puppy or dog to her new home. Although everyone has visions of the perfect homecoming and a family that lives happily ever after, this isn't always the case. Careful consideration of your puppy and her new environment, however, can help make the transition go as smoothly as possible.

Mixing babies and Jack Russells

Introducing your puppy or dog to a newborn usually can be accomplished smoothly and easily, especially if the newborn is already in the house and the puppy or dog is the newcomer. In this case, the dog has few expectations of who is higher in the hierarchy than she is and will accept all house-dwellers as part of her new home. She will be looking for ways to fit in and will be most open to training and imprinting in her first few days in the house.

Preparing your dog

If you're bringing a newborn home to a puppy or dog already in the household, you need to take a few extra steps to let your terrier know that she's not being replaced and that she's still very much loved and wanted. The easiest way to do this is to prepare your dog in advance for the baby's homecoming.

WARNING

Hard as it may be, don't be overly protective of your newborn. Chasing your dog away whenever she gets close to the baby only breeds resentment in your dog and may lead to aggressive behavior toward you or your baby.

All dogs have an acute sense of smell, and they learn much about their surroundings by using their noses. Your first step, before baby gets close to coming home, should be to bring home a blanket or a piece of clothing the baby has worn. Let the dog smell the clothing and grow accustomed to this new scent over a day or two. If possible, bring home one of the baby's swaddling blankets and place it in your Jack Russell's bed for her to sleep with a few days prior to your homecoming. This makes your terrier comfortable with the scent of your new little one and is a non-threatening way to begin the introduction.

TRY THIS

During this time, play a recording of the newborn's cry as your spouse or another family member pets and reassures your terrier. This prevents your Jack Russell from going nuts every time your baby wakes up and cries, and will help your JRT grow accustomed to this new loud noise in her home. Watching programs on TV or videotapes that show babies crying also will help disarm your dog. Soon she will take a baby's cry in stride and won't become anxious at the noise.

Home from the hospital

When you finally bring your newborn home, let the father hold the baby while the mother welcomes the dog. She should scratch and pet the dog, letting her know that Mom is very happy to be home and is equally happy to see her beloved Jack Russell. After a few minutes, Dad can hand the baby back to Mom; he, too, should make a bit of a fuss about seeing the JRT again. Resist the temptation to rush this step. It could easily be the key to either your success or your failure. The main thing is to make your Jack Russell feel that, in spite of the new bundle, she still has a place of importance in the family.

TIP

Let your Jack Russell sniff, touch, and even nuzzle your newborn while you stay alert so she doesn't try to jump or get too rough. A terrier who is familiar with a baby is more likely to accept and even protect the child. Place the baby in your arms and let your dog look at the baby and smell his blankets and clothing. Because you've already introduced your baby's scent to your Jack Russell, the dog won't be totally taken off guard by this new intrusion. Let your dog be curious, look, and gently touch, but don't allow her to jump on the chair or couch with you. Remember your awe and curiosity at seeing this new little being for the first time? Your Jack Russell feels the same way. She simply wants to see what this new little bundle is and to know that her place isn't being threatened by your new addition.

Pet and talk to your Jack Russell — or even feed her small cookies or treats — while holding the baby. This shows the dog that she's still a cherished part of your home and that she shouldn't be threatened by the baby. Allow your terrier into the baby's room with you, but only when you're in the room. By making it pleasant for your JRT to be around the baby, the dog will come to associate the baby with good things and will look forward to being with him. Spend some extra time reassuring your dog during this period of transition, and she'll be more willing to welcome your new baby as a positive addition to the family.

When I brought my newborn home to our two terriers, I followed all the preceding steps. I was shocked to find that, not only did my two terriers adore our new baby, they were bound and determined to protect her at all costs — even from each other! The dog who followed me into the baby's room first wouldn't let the other one in, and whenever she would cry, both would come running to make sure no one was threatening their "baby sister." If you've ever doubted the intelligence of these dogs, watch them in action and your doubts will be put to rest forever. They are truly amazing little animals!

Mixing tiny tots and terriers

Introducing a young child to a new dog is easier than bringing a new baby home for the first time. Because the dog is in a new environment, she will be curious about her new surroundings. She won't be threatened by your children's attentions, provided they don't overwhelm her or try to intimidate her by poking or teasing. The success of this introduction rests solely on your children. If the new dog feels welcome and comfortable, all will go well. If your new addition to the family feels threatened and frightened, she will react either by tucking her tail and hiding in her crate or by turning to aggression to protect herself.

TIP

Discuss the rules of the road with your children and set up guidelines before you bring the puppy home. Jack Russells make nice pets for children (see Figure 6-3), provided the children aren't allowed to abuse or tease the terrier.

FIGURE 6-3:
Children and JRTs can get along beautifully.

© Nance Photography/AKC Stock Images

Keep the moment mellow

Children often are so excited about having a new puppy that they scream or shriek at the puppy's every move. This is likely to frighten a new puppy in totally foreign surroundings, and the dog will probably head for the nearest corner or dark spot. Talk to your children and let them know they should make the puppy feel welcome by gently petting her and by not making noises that could frighten her. If your children are old enough to understand logic, they usually will be quite willing to tone down their excitement if they realize the puppy is scared. Ask your children to talk to the puppy in a quiet voice and to keep their movements slow and purposeful. Show them how to gently pet the puppy and how the puppy likes to play with balls and chew toys on the ground.

Pickin' up the pup

Remember that young children are notoriously clumsy with items they hold, and they often drop whatever is in their clutches. For this reason, don't let a young child pick the puppy off the ground. If the child accidentally drops her, the puppy could be injured or, at the very least, frightened. How would you like to be dropped on your head on a first date? You would never go out with that person again and would likely avoid any further encounters at all costs. The same is true of your puppy. If you drop her even one time, she's unlikely to be as forthcoming with her affections in the future.

If your young child wants to hold the puppy, have him sit on the floor and hold the puppy on his lap. An adult or older child always should be present when your child holds your puppy to make sure he is holding her gently and isn't unduly restraining her. The child also should be taught to keep his hands and face away from the puppy's mouth to avoid injury. Puppies have sharp little teeth and aren't always choosy about what they bite down on. An excited puppy is likely to playfully snap or nip. If your youngster's face is in the dog's line of sight, the child could receive a nasty bite.

Supervise!

Keep a close eye on both the puppy and your children after your terrier comes home. You need to make sure your children don't forget that the puppy is a living, breathing creature that has to be handled gently. It's easy for them to slip back into thinking a puppy is a stuffed animal that can be dropped or hurled across the room like their stuffed toys. Obviously, this can result in serious injury to your new puppy or can lead to aggressive behavior to protect herself. Remind your children to treat the puppy as a new playmate that has feelings of her own and to be very gentle when playing with their new dog. Encourage them to think of your new puppy as a member of the family and enforce the same "no biting, no hitting" rules as if your JRT were another child.

It's a crate life!

A crate can be very helpful during this time of transition. The crate gives your puppy a safe place to be when she begins to feel overwhelmed, and it enables you to put the puppy someplace that is labeled off-limits to the children. This will keep both your sanity and that of your terrier intact. Make the crate a homey place for your pup by placing a soft, fuzzy blanket at the bottom and by providing fresh water and food plus a chew toy or two for the puppy to amuse herself if she so desires. The crate should be roomy, but it shouldn't be so large that the puppy has room to run around. See Chapters 7 and 9 for more information about using a crate.

When your puppy is playing with your children, give her free access to her crate by leaving the door open. This way, if your terrier feels threatened, she easily can retreat to her comfortable cubbyhole. By letting the children know that the crate is off-limits, your puppy can feel safe and can choose when she wants to come out to play. This keeps the puppy from feeling cornered with no place to go, and it teaches your children how to read your JRT's actions.

Introducing your JRT to another dog

The success of introducing a puppy or dog into a household that already has a dog or cat depends greatly on the attitude of the other pet. Some pets get very possessive of their family and would rather not share that attention with an intruder. Some even resort to violent behavior to try to chase off the new pet. This especially is common with older dogs or cats who have had the run of the house and family for many years. They have grown accustomed to their lifestyle and are unlikely to welcome a dramatic change.

Try to see the situation from your other pet's point of view. For months or even years, the pet has had your family's attention all to herself and is secure in knowing that her needs will be met. She can sleep and play when she wants and never has to share her food, water, or toys with anyone else. Suddenly, this interloper shows up and starts sniffing around her food dish and getting loads of attention from members of the family. The older pet feels insecure, not knowing whether her place within the family is still intact. Like any threatened animal, she responds by protecting her territory and by trying to run off the offending addition. Some dogs even resort to violence to protect what they feel are their rights. It's up to you to play referee and to ease your pet's anxieties during this difficult time.

REMEMBER

It is more difficult for an older JRT to adjust to another adult dog than to a younger dog. Keep this in mind when selecting a dog for your family. If an older dog or cat already is present, opt for a puppy or a young dog as your new pet.

Easy does it!

You can lessen these anxious feelings by slowly introducing your puppy to your other pets. You don't like to be forced into actions against your will and neither does your pet. Likewise, your pet will resent lengthy introductions and forced periods of play. Allow the relationship to develop slowly, and you'll have much better success in the long run.

To start out, let your pet have the run of her usual area (whether a yard, a room, or the whole house) and restrict the puppy to one area of the home that is all her own. Keep their feeding areas well separated and spend time alone with each so they both feel wanted and secure. When things have settled down a bit, you can bring the puppy and the other pet into the living room or into the yard for supervised time together, allowing each one to explore the other. Allow both pets to approach each other in their own time and in their own way. They will be curious about one another, and the older pet likely will show signs of dominance toward the puppy.

Watch carefully

Don't try to play referee unless the situation really gets out of hand. It's best to let the animals work it out between themselves, provided no one is in serious danger. Letting your puppy get smacked in the nose a time or two by the cat will teach the puppy that the cat has claws and should be respected. Likewise, letting your excited pup get pinned down or snapped at by an older dog will teach her to back off when the dog growls. The puppy then will be more likely to give your older dog a wide berth in the future. If things do start to get out of hand, startle both pets by making a loud noise and then separate them until another day. If you gradually increase the time they spend together, they will become friends (or at least tolerable cohabitants) in no time.

WARNING

Don't force your older dog to approach your new puppy by placing her on a leash and dragging her over or by locking the two in an enclosed space together. Not only will the older pet resent the introduction, she will resent you, as well. Instead, let them approach each other whenever they're ready and be close by to intervene if things get nasty.

WARNING

Avoid the temptation to put your pets together before spending some quality, supervised time with them to judge their reactions. Although a cat is likely to hit the high road and escape to places your puppy can't reach, another dog is likely to turn on your new puppy and act aggressively, sometimes causing injury. Even after a day or two of playing nicely together, the relationship can go downhill. Don't assume that, because they've been tolerant of each other for a day or two, everything is fine. Spending a few days supervising your pets will prevent possible injuries and vet bills. Don't rush the process. The pets will make progress in their own time and in their own way.

Even after they've adjusted to each other, keep their feeding areas separate to prevent fights over food and treats. If you give treats by hand, make sure each dog gets an equal amount and don't play favorites. Playing favorites builds resentment and erodes any trust your pets may be building together. Give them treats in their respective dishes and avoid hand-feeding for a while. Be sure to spend plenty of time with each pet, and remember that abundant exercise will help keep tempers in check.

Being cautious with feline foes

Cats can pose a problem if your JRT is more than two years old when you bring her home. I know of many JRT puppies that were successfully raised in a kitty household; they were able to adjust and learn respect for the cats. Most adult Jack Russells who have not previously been exposed to cats, however, view cats as prey and try to hunt and kill them.

Male JRTs seem to be especially aggressive toward cats, but I have known several females that were just as intent on stalking other animals. The JRT was meant to hunt. No amount of punishment will change the basic temperament of the breed. If you have a cat you want to stick around, avoid bringing an older JRT into the home. It would be a tragedy to lose a pet over a preventable mistake.

REMEMBERING THE RAT AND GUINEA PIG FETISH

If you look at the breeding and evolution of the Jack Russell Terrier (see Chapter 2), you can see that they were, first and foremost, hunting dogs entrusted with tracking foxes and with keeping stables clear of rats and other rodents. With this in mind, it is easy to see why a Guinea pig or a domestic rat is a lousy match for a new Jack Russell Terrier. Try as you may to make these two become friends, your JRT is more likely to view your small, furry friend as her next meal.

Hunting rodents has been inbred into these terriers for hundreds of years. No amount of training will ever truly rid the JRT of her desire to hunt and to destroy anything that smells even remotely like a rodent. Instead of setting yourself up for heartache, it is best to avoid mixing these two very different beasts. Guinea pigs, rats, mice, rabbits, ferrets, and even snakes all should be avoided if you plan to have a JRT in your household. Otherwise, you could come home to a dead rat and a smiling terrier when you least expect it.

Even if you keep the rodent in another room or high out of reach, your terrier could find a way to penetrate the barriers you set up. Remember that Jack Russells are crafty little dogs and have remarkable jumping abilities. They also are great demolition dogs and can claw and bite their way through even the toughest cage. Add to this a persistence bordering on obsession that's unmatched by any other breed, and you will see that having one of these pets in the house or a surrounding area is a bad idea. It may not happen right away, but sooner or later, your Jack Russell will find a way to make relish out of your rat or make gumbo out of your Guinea pig.

If you're introducing your new puppy to an older cat, make sure that the cat has plenty of room to retreat away from the puppy and that the cat is allowed to approach at his own rate. Don't punish the cat for slapping your puppy in the nose. The puppy must learn that the cat has claws and isn't another play toy. If the puppy seems to overly excited, separate the two for a while and then try the introduction again. By letting the two approach each other at will, both will feel they are in control of the situation. They will be less likely to turn aggressive, at least beyond a hiss or a bark.

Chapter **7**

House-training Your Jack Russell

Perhaps the most frustrating training task you will embark upon with your Jack Russell is house-training. Why, you may ask? The answer is simple. Although JRTs are extremely intelligent and learn very quickly, they also can be strong-willed. Because your dog has an agenda of his own, he may not readily accept your version of how life should be.

TRY THIS

To keep this problem from arising, start training your JRT the moment you get him home. This helps set the ground rules right from the beginning and starts you on your way to house-training success. Keep in mind, however, that you may do all the right things but still have a hard time with this seemingly simple task. Don't despair. Many Jack Russell owners have walked down this frustrating path before you. Rest assured that almost all eventually ended up with a properly house-trained dog. It can take up to six or even eight months, however, so be patient.

REMEMBER

Keep a positive attitude when house-training your puppy. Keep in mind that it takes years for a human baby to learn to use the toilet, yet people expect puppies to learn discipline and control in just a few short months. The more positive your attitude toward house-training, the quicker your puppy will respond.

Getting Started

Depending on how old your puppy is when you get him, he may not be physically ready to be completely house-trained. Most puppies come home to their new families when they're eight to ten weeks of age. At this stage, they are unable to control their bladder for an entire night and must relieve themselves every few hours. If your puppy is younger than six months old when you bring him home, be sympathetic to the fact that you may be asking him to do something he's physically incapable of doing. Does this mean you should wait until your puppy is six months old to begin house-training? Absolutely not! But it does mean that, mentally, you need to be prepared for less-than-perfect compliance for a while until your puppy understands what you're asking of him and until he can physically control his functions to comply with your wishes.

Selecting an indoor confinement area

Before you bring your puppy home, select a place where he will be kept at night. It should be a place that can be readily closed off, that's small enough to be manageable, and that has an easy-to-clean floor. This will be your puppy's bedroom, at least until house-training is well on its way to being a habit. You need to purchase a crate for your puppy, and you should plan ahead to have lots of newspaper or house-training pads on hand. You can purchase house-training pads from most pet stores in your area. They have a water-resistant backing and are scented to tempt your puppy to eliminate on the pads instead of on the floor or the rug. Either newspapers or pads will work, but puppy pads are easier to clean up. On the other hand, they also are more expensive.

Making a lot of potty trips

Someone needs to stay with the puppy for the first few days he resides with you. Taking a week off from work really is the best idea. If someone is available to watch your puppy for signs that he needs to go out and can immediately take him outside to eliminate, the chances for more immediate success increase. If, however, he is left to his own devices as to when and where to eliminate, it will take longer to train your puppy to eliminate outside. He will incorrectly assume that other places in the house are acceptable alternatives to his outside toilet.

REMEMBER

The more often you can catch your puppy before he eliminates in the house and can take him outside to do his business, the more quickly he will associate outside and grass with going potty. This is a situation in which success invariably breeds success. The dog also will be more willing to go when it's convenient for you.

Using a crate

TRY THIS

The crate truly is one of the best inventions on the market for dog training and is an invaluable tool for house-training. Although you may be inclined to look at a crate and think, "I can't possibly lock up my poor puppy in that thing," keep in mind that your puppy will view his crate as a comforting refuge rather than as a jail. This only is true, however, if you use the crate as a training tool and not as a method of punishment. A puppy likes to curl up in cozy corners. He feels safe in his little refuge and views it as a place all his own. As long as your puppy sees his crate as a positive place to be, he will look forward to curling up within his comforting confines.

After a puppy learns that his crate is his personal cubbyhole, he will respect that space as his bed. This means the puppy's natural instinct will be to keep the bed clean. As long as your puppy isn't forced to wait longer than his immature bladder can endure, he will be willing and grateful to have an alternate and more appropriate place to relieve himself (such as outside). By providing an "escape" from his den, you will keep intact your puppy's natural instinct not to soil his bed — this ultimately will help you in your house- training goals.

WARNING

Don't leave your very young puppy in a crate all night with no place to relieve himself. This forces your puppy to soil his bed, making both of you unhappy. It also can cause problems in the future with house-training. Dogs naturally eliminate away from their beds, but if your puppy has no choice but to soil his bed, this instinct is diminished. Keep the crate in or near enough to your bedroom so that you can hear him cry when he has to go out. Close him in it at night and get up to take him outside if he cries in the middle of the night. Most puppies can "hold it" throughout the night by the time they're 10 to 12 weeks old.

REMEMBER

When shopping for your puppy's crate, make sure you don't buy one that's too large. If your puppy has loads of room to move around, he will use a corner of the crate to relieve himself, thinking that the corner is far enough away from his bed.

TRY THIS

Both after he eats or when he first wakes up are good times to catch your puppy in the act and advance your house-training goals. Be sure to pay close attention to his actions after a good round of play or if you know it has been a while since he last took a potty break. When, through either luck on his part or vigilance on yours, he goes outside as requested, give him lots of hugs and treats to signal that you're very pleased with his progress.

BATTLE OF THE SEXES

For many reasons, male dogs seem to be more difficult to house-train than their female counterparts. The primary reason for this behavior is found in the male dog's natural instinct to mark his territory as a warning to other male dogs as well as to attract potential mates. To alleviate this problem, you may want to consider neutering your male puppy as soon as the veterinarian gives you the okay. This will catch your puppy early enough in his development to prevent this habit from becoming established or at least before it is firmly ingrained in his behavior.

If you wait too long to have your puppy neutered, he may urinate on your furniture, plastic bags, clothing, bedding, or any number of leg-height objects in an attempt to warn other male dogs that these places are within his denning area. Although this is great for warding off other male dogs, it doesn't usually sit well with you, the home-owner, who has to clean up all the puddles. The benefits and drawbacks of spaying and neutering are discussed in Chapter 10, but trust me on this one — a neutered male is much more pleasant to be around than an intact one.

As your puppy comes to understand that relieving himself outside is rewarding to him and it's where you want him to go, he will accept house-training and will begin to signal you that he needs to go outside by going to the door or by acting anxious. This is a big step for a puppy, and you must be sure to praise and reward this effort with lots of love. As soon as you notice one of these signs (circling and sniffing are typical), take your puppy outside immediately and attempt to get him to relieve himself. When he does, reward him as before with lots of praise and treats. As the behavior is reinforced, so is your puppy's desire to be rewarded, cementing your house-training efforts.

REMEMBER

Don't assume that, just because your puppy has had a particularly successful week, he's fully house-trained. Even the best learners have setbacks. Expect mistakes to happen and deal with them calmly and without anger.

Making Adjustments

Even after your pup has learned to signal when he wants to go out, he still will have accidents. No one is perfect, and this applies to your puppy as well. Many factors can contribute to your puppy's lapse in control. A visitor to your house, for example, may overstimulate him. He may become so excited at the sight of a new person that he loses his ability to control his bladder. A long or rambunctious bout of playing or roughhousing may also distract your puppy long enough that he

80   PART 3 **Setting Out the Welcome Mat**

forgets he has to control himself and go outside. Your puppy plays and plays and, before he realizes it's past time to go, is caught with a full bladder and doesn't have enough time or self-control to hold it in. The result is a wet spot on the carpet. All these scenarios can be prevented with a bit of planning and attention on your part.

REMEMBER

If an accident happens, it's the owner's fault, not the puppy's. Always keep a puppy who isn't fully house-trained confined to a pen or crate, leashed or tethered, or under the immediate and direct supervision of a responsible adult or older child. As your puppy learns to control his bladder and bowels, he can be gradually given more freedom. If he starts having accidents, the owner has given him too much freedom too soon.

Spotting the patterns

To avoid accidents, remember that puppies have patterns they tend to follow. These patterns can help you predict the most likely times to further your house-training. Your puppy will need to urinate as soon as he wakes up from a nap or in the morning and immediately following intense play. Drinking a lot of water all at once is a sign that a potty break is soon to follow. A recent meal or bout of excitement also can signal the need for relief.

REMEMBER

Don't always wait for your puppy to show signs that he's about to have an accident. If you take your puppy out immediately after these events occur, your puppy likely will be quite ready to do his business wherever he happens to be. By preempting your puppy's needs, he will think that going outside is his idea. He will be more likely to continue to do so whenever the opportunity presents itself.

WARNING

If your dog begins eating his stools (called *coprophagia*) or those of another dog, call your vet. This habit may be a sign of improper digestion or a chemical imbalance that causes undigested food to be left in the stool. It may also be the result of boredom or stress. Although not life threatening, this unpleasant habit is best caught early.

Being aware of your puppy's schedule enables you to create circumstances conducive to successful house-training. If you're alert to your puppy's signals that he needs to "go," you soon learn that he has a predictable pattern. By using this pattern, you can predict when your puppy most likely is ready to go outside. Don't wait for an accident to occur or almost occur. Take the initiative by predicting when your puppy needs to go and take him outside before he even is aware of the need.

CLEANING UP QUICKLY

If your puppy has an accident, immediately clean the spot and thoroughly deodorize the area. Puppies tend to relieve themselves in areas that smell like previous "potty spots." By eliminating the odor, you reduce the possibility of your puppy visiting the same location. Vinegar and water work well, as do many nonammonia cleansers. You may also want to try an enzyme-based cleaner such as Nature's Miracle.

The quicker you get to the scene of the accident, the smaller the chance a permanent odor will set — so act quickly. Better yet, keep your eyes open for signs of an impending accident and avoid it in the first place.

Recognizing bathroom body language

To determine your puppy's pattern, pay attention to his body language. Usually, a puppy circles an area several times, sniffing or whining, before settling on a spot to relieve himself. If you notice this behavior in time, you can take your puppy either outside or to the paper and let him know that this is where you want him to do his business. If the puppy complies, abundant praise and treats must quickly follow.

Getting caught in the act

Even if your puppy starts to relieve himself in the house, you still can save the situation if you act quickly. Calmly pick up your puppy saying "No!" and take him outside. Your puppy will be startled enough to stop in midstream (usually) and will let you take him outside without a problem. Most of the time, your puppy still will have to relieve himself and will comply by doing so outside. Again, heap on the praise and let him know that he has done well. Adding a treat or two never hurts.

TIP

Whenever you take your puppy outside to eliminate and he goes on command, be sure to praise him emphatically by petting him, saying "Good dog," and giving him a treat. This reinforces that you're pleased with your puppy's actions and encourages him to repeat his performance next time.

Avoiding common house-training mistakes

Contrary to numerous books available on the subject (many of which are out-dated), rubbing a dog's nose in his urine or feces doesn't promote house-training. Neither does hitting a dog or puppy with a rolled newspaper if he has an accident. These reactions only breed fear and resentment in your terrier and may also lead to aggression from your puppy. If he feels threatened enough, he may try to fight back to protect himself, and you could inadvertently create a biter.

Another possible effect of overzealous punishment is that it teaches your dog not to relieve himself in your presence. Some dogs "learn" that to eliminate at all is unsafe — now you have a real problem. This creates a puppy who either soils in the house when you're away or is afraid to relieve himself in front of you, whether you're inside or outside. Both scenarios are counterproductive to your house-training goals. To be successful, you must be able to observe your puppy doing it right to quickly follow up with praise. If this opportunity is taken away, your training will take significantly longer. Keep this in mind when you're tempted to lose your cool and resort to punishment.

Becoming Perfect with Practice

I can't stress enough the importance of consistent training with your puppy or dog. If your puppy gets away with a bad behavior even once, he will continue to try for the exception rather than the rule. It is your job as trainer to set the boundaries, to make sure your puppy understands the rules and to make sure these rules are followed. This means monitoring your dog each and every day. If you allow the rules to be broken just once, they are likely to be broken again.

If you forget to praise your puppy, he will see little value in complying with your wishes in the future. Likewise, if you allow your puppy to be rewarded for unacceptable behavior even once, you're encouraging him to continue that behavior. If you're unable to consistently watch your puppy through certain times of the house-training phase, place him outside or in a confined area and be patient if he doesn't do everything exactly right. House-training takes time even in the best of situations. If your time to devote to training is limited, understand that it will take your puppy longer to really understand what is expected of him. He is, after all, just a baby.

Your purpose as a Jack Russell Terrier owner is to make your puppy feels wanted and loved, not rejected or shunned. You wouldn't hit a baby for going to the bathroom in her diaper, and the same rules should apply to your baby dog. Like babies, puppies and adult dogs need consistent, positive reinforcement which, in the long run, is much more rewarding and effective.

REMEMBER

When all else fails and you're at the end of your rope, remember this: No matter how smart the trainer, how precocious the puppy or how vigilant you may be, most Jack Russells aren't fully house-trained until they are at least six months old, and some take even longer. Just keep your chin up, your temper in check, and treats on hand, and you eventually will succeed. I promise!

Chapter **8**

Obedience Training Your JRT

The Jack Russell Terrier has a distinct personality with strong opinions about who he is and how things should be run. There are times when you and your JRT will have differences of opinion about how a situation should be handled, and your terrier will use his not-insignificant mental capacities to avoid your rules or to conveniently forget that there are any rules to follow in the first place. As a trainer, it then becomes your job to see that the rules are once again firmly established — without losing your temper or your sanity.

You also must remember that training your Jack Russell Terrier will be far from easy. With a breed as smart as the JRT, you'd think training would be a breeze, but this simply isn't the case. Because they're so smart, they also have strong opinions as to the behaviors they prefer. You should know, however, that your JRT will be a much happier dog after he understands the rules. These rules provide structure in your terrier's life and create a feeling of stability that results from knowing what's expected of him from day to day. You can't lose your patience, however, or your training sessions will be dismal failures.

REMEMBER

Be realistic when setting rules for your terrier. A young puppy has physical limitations on his bodily functions, and asking too much of him too soon causes frustration for both you and your pet. Remember, too, that JRTs aren't mellow dogs. Asking your terrier to lie at your feet for hours on end simply isn't reasonable.

Establishing Boundaries and Rules

From the day your puppy comes home, set boundaries and rules for your terrier to follow. Dogs, and especially Jack Russells, do well with guidelines that keep their lives neat and orderly. Without these guidelines, havoc and chaos would eventually rule, making everyone in the household — including your terrier — absolutely crazy. Of course, a young puppy will have fewer "rules" than an older puppy, and an older puppy will not be held to the same standards as an adult dog.

REMEMBER

Keep in mind that these are only guidelines. No dog is perfect; they all have lapses in memory and judgment somewhere along the way. Getting angry only frustrates both you and your terrier and leads to unrealistic expectations and goals for both of you.

From day one, your Jack Russell Terrier must understand that you are the benevolent leader in the household, and he is not. If you create this relationship when the puppy is young, it is much easier to continue throughout older life and training. If you're lulled into the fantasy that the puppy is so cute and that his little habits like gnawing on your slippers or ignoring your commands are so endearing, you're setting yourself up for some serious problems when you begin obedience training with your dog.

The best time to set the record straight is the moment your puppy comes home. Inappropriate behaviors should be ignored, and appropriate behaviors should be rewarded. JRTs don't do well with punishment and often retaliate with very deliberate and well-thought-out acts of defiance such as wetting on your pillow or bed in the middle of the night or chewing up your favorite slippers the day after your disagreement. Punishment can often lead to a more aggressive dog or, conversely, to a dog who cowers whenever you lift a hand and who's more likely to run when called than to come to you.

REMEMBER

You reward appropriate behaviors and prevent inappropriate ones. Your dog isn't bad; he's simply made a behavioral mistake!

Becoming the leader of the pack

Remember that dogs naturally work in packs. This translates to teamwork. The strength of a hunting pack of coyotes is that they can rely on one another to surround their prey, making it easier to bring home dinner. Your domesticated puppy has the same frame of mind. He needs to know who is the leader of the pack (you), who are the higher-ranked dogs (your family), and what his role is within your pack (your household). By providing a structured environment in which your puppy understands his role and the rules of the pack, he will gladly work with the team to make a successful relationship.

REMEMBER

When training your Jack Russell Terrier, you must remember that he comes from a very smart breed of dog. Although you need to set the terms of the relationship, be sure that you go into it with the understanding that you must train your terrier and not dominate him. This distinction is a fine line. Your JRT must respect you and must understand that you're the head of the household, but he shouldn't fear or be intimidated by you.

Take care to increase your terrier's experiences by exposing him to the correct stimuli and by teaching him what you want. You may become frustrated with training your Jack Russell and may be tempted to use force, but this will only be counterproductive. A dog who's fearful is unlikely to want to learn and will be reluctant to participate in training sessions. A terrier who truly loves and respects his owner bends over backward — sometimes literally — to learn a skill and puts his mental energies into learning rather than evading.

TIP

Don't be afraid to use your Jack Russell's drive for food, such as cookies and treats, to reward your puppy. Food can be a good way to reinforce a desired behavior, as is rewarding your Jack Russell Terrier with quick rounds of play with his favorite toy whenever he has done a particularly good job of behaving himself.

Have you ever heard the expression that you catch more flies with honey than you do with vinegar? This holds true tenfold for your JRT. Eager to learn and be rewarded, these dogs will go to the ends of the earth for you if they understand what's expected of them. After that trust is broken, however, it is virtually impossible to regain.

Being consistent in your training

How do you set the rules without breaking your dog's spirit? Consistency. By consistently using the same commands and by consistently rewarding your terrier when he performs correctly, you can create consistency in your dog's responses. If your terrier learns that unwanted behaviors are rewarding, he will look for opportunities to repeat those behaviors. If unwanted behaviors aren't rewarded, those behaviors will stop. And if appropriate behaviors are rewarded, your JRT will repeat those behaviors, too.

You can't be passive in your terrier's training and hope that your dog will intuit appropriate behaviors from inappropriate. Sometimes, much to your dismay, you will physically have to get out off the couch to accomplish your desired objective. Sometimes this means you have to physically go over to your terrier, pick him up, and bring him to you when you ask him to come. Sometimes you have to physically move your dog into his bed for a timeout after he's been bad. Understand that this is all part of the training process. If you take the time to do it right when your dog's a puppy, your training will be much less tiresome and time-consuming than when your puppy is a grown dog.

Perfecting your timing

TIP

Try to catch your puppy doing something right or responding correctly to a command and reward him when he behaves. This can be a simple "Good dog!" with lots of pats and scratches, or it can be a small cookie or dog bone to emphasize the point.

Be sure to immediately reward correct behavior when he responds to a command. If you see your puppy starting to wet on the carpet or chewing on something off-limits, give the command "No!" If your puppy stops, reward him! He has torn his attention away from either Mother Nature or a very tempting tidbit, and this is quite a commendable task for a puppy. He is showing that you deserve to be listened to and that he respects your voice. This is a big step, and rewards at that moment go a long way toward building respect and the desire to please in the future.

Setting Your Sights on Obedience Training

Contrary to popular belief, Jack Russell Terriers can be trained quite effectively. It takes patience, understanding, and behavior management, however, and the sooner you start training your terrier, the easier time you'll have. This is why I recommend that all new terrier owners enroll in a basic obedience course with their puppies as soon as the puppy is old enough to walk on a leash and to stay focused for a decent amount of time. This usually occurs when the puppy is around ten weeks old. Obedience training can help with the following:

>> **Setting goals:** An obedience training class is important for many reasons. First, it gives you and your puppy a goal to work toward together, and it provides a strong support group if you start to get frustrated with your puppy's progress (or lack of progress!). The class instructor can be a valuable resource, not only for training tips and ideas but for suggestions of how to have fun with your dog. The instructor also can provide health and grooming tips to keep your puppy fit and healthy.

>> **Staying focused:** By enrolling in a structured class setting, you're making a commitment to your new puppy to get out with him regularly and to devote a portion of your time to his training. You're less likely to quit midstream if you've spent hard-earned dollars to sign up for the class, and you'll also be more apt to practice at home if you have someone giving you homework assignments and checking your progress on a regular basis.

>> **Finding emotional support:** As an added benefit, you have a place to ask questions and to vent frustrations should the lessons prove to be more challenging than you anticipated. This one-on-one personal touch is much easier than looking up information in a book every time you get frustrated with a specific behavior that your puppy has invented, seemingly just to thwart you.

>> **Socialization:** By attending a class with others, your puppy learns to socialize around both people and dogs.

>> **Charting your progress:** You receive guidance regarding which lessons and tasks are appropriate for your puppy's age and development, and you may not be as tempted to ask something of your puppy that he isn't developmentally prepared to do. Your instructor can shed some light on your puppy's physical and mental limitations at each stage of the game and will guide you through the increasingly difficult stages of training as your puppy is ready and able to accept them. This allows your puppy to master skills as he matures, and it provides a solid framework of acceptable behavior without becoming overly frustrated or bored. It also helps to teach your puppy social skills because he will be repeatedly asked to interact with the other puppies in the group and will be less likely to be an overaggressive terrier.

Teaching Commands

TRY THIS

Before discussing the basic commands that every puppy should master (covered in the following sections), I first look at some hints for training success. By understanding how your puppy thinks and learns, you can make your short training sessions effective and fun for your puppy.

>> **Train before meals.** Plan to hold your training sessions before the puppy eats a big meal. This encourages your puppy to be active, and allows you to more effectively use treats in your training session. After a puppy eats, his system slows down. This leads to a more lethargic dog who isn't as motivated by food. It also gives you an opportunity to make the connection between training and something pleasurable, like food.

>> **Gather up the goods.** Always make sure you have the proper equipment on hand to have a productive training session. This should include a harness, a strong 6-foot leash, a 20-foot lightweight lead, and plenty of cookies or treats. I prefer a harness on smaller puppies because they're less likely to choke themselves and to create inadvertent corrections (see Chapter 9 for details). An older dog does well with a lightweight chain or a leather choke collar,

although keep in mind that, despite this name, the intention of this collar is to correct, not to choke. Let the puppy wear his harness or collar around the house for a week or two (always while supervised) so that he gets accustomed to the feel of having something on this neck or body. Never leave a choke collar on an unattended dog.

>> **Less is more.** Keep your training sessions short (ten minutes) and productive. Always end on a good note and don't be tempted to overschool a trick or a command. Your puppy gets bored easily, and several very short sessions will be much more productive in the long run than a few long sessions. Also make sure your sessions are fun and entertaining for your puppy. You want him to look forward to training, not head for the hills the moment he sees you coming.

>> **Keep it simple.** Give your puppy simple commands that aren't more than one or two words long. Use your puppy's name before giving a command to get his attention and then give the command in a strong, clear voice. The command should be given before you move your puppy into action so the puppy learns the sequence of command-response. Always use exactly the same word for a requested action. Puppies get confused easily, so keep your puppy's new vocabulary short and concise. And always remember to reward or treat for each and every positive response. The reward doesn't always have to be food, though in the beginning this system is highly effective. As your puppy ages, pats on the head and scratches should replace some of the treats, but treats should never be eliminated entirely.

>> **Accentuate the positive.** Remember that you're engaged in a training session, not an intimidation session. Keep all of your commands and responses positive. If you ask your puppy to sit and he ignores you, guide your puppy into a sit position and reward your puppy as if he did it on his own. You should view your training as requests and rewards — punishment never should enter the picture. Make sure you reward the desired response, performed either voluntarily or with your help, each and every time you give the command, and be patient with your puppy's learning process.

>> **Consistency is the key.** Say what you mean and mean what you say. Although you should be focused on a training session, some of the behaviors a young terrier comes up with are undeniably cute. Don't allow yourself to be diverted from the command at hand just because your terrier has devised a particularly fetching avoidance technique. Likewise, don't train only when it is convenient for you. If you don't want your dog to jump on you, you must manage his behavior to prevent his jumping on you and reward him for not jumping — even if your hands are full or the phone is ringing. Consistency is the golden rule in dog training.

>> **Be patient.** Remember that your puppy won't always be in the mood for training. There will be times when, try as you may, you simply can't get anything worthwhile accomplished. Accept this fact and don't pressure yourself or your puppy to make giant steps forward during every training session. Sometimes your puppy needs to mull things over a little, and what seemed like an unproductive training session magically resolves itself the next time around. Regardless of how small the progress, always end on a positive note and always keep your training times fun.

TIP

Stand up straight when giving your puppy his commands. When you bend over to your terrier's level, it looks more like an invitation to play. This shifts his concentration toward listening to the commands and taking them seriously.

REMEMBER

Puppies and dogs learn best through repetition. Every time a command and response is repeated, the puppy learns to connect one with the other. Remember, however, that this can be a bad thing as well as a good thing. If you inadvertently reward your puppy's unwanted behavior with attention, even negative attention, you're teaching your puppy that unwanted behavior gets him noticed.

Sitting pretty

The sit command is fairly easy to teach and is one of the most useful commands in your puppy's repertoire. Because it is easy to teach and is easy for your terrier to understand, it is a good command to use in early obedience training. Here's how:

TRY THIS

1. **Place your puppy on your left side next to your leg and encourage him to look up at you by saying his name.**

2. **In a firm, clear voice, give the command, "Sit."**

3. **Hold a treat just above your puppy's eye level to get him to look up, thus lowering his rump.**

   This naturally and easily puts the puppy's body into an almost-sitting position. All you have to do then is help the process along with the vocal command.

4. **As soon as your puppy sits, praise him and give him a treat.**

TIP

As your puppy begins to get the idea, require a more complete sit on his own before handing over the treat. Soon your puppy will be sitting like a pro (and possibly even sitting up like a gopher) to get his favorite treat.

Come hither yon terrier

Teaching your puppy to come is one of the most important fundamentals of training. It should be easy for you and for your puppy. Why? Because you practice daily without even realizing it. When you feed your puppy or when you come home from work and meet him at the door, you're calling your puppy by name and rewarding him when he comes to you, either through praise or through food. Very soon, your puppy learns that, whenever he responds to his name, he will get either petted, fed, or taken outside to play or relieve himself, all of which are viewed as positive events by your puppy.

TIP

Don't call your terrier to you with the come command for something unpleasant, such as giving your puppy a bath or giving him a pill. This only teaches your puppy to run the other way when you call. If you have to bathe your puppy, pick him up and carry him to the bathing area.

TRY THIS

Getting your puppy to come when he's outdoors and surrounded by many other distractions is considerably more difficult than getting his attention around the home, but it's an important response. It could even save your puppy's life. Be sure to reward each and every effort your puppy makes to respond correctly to the come command and try to make your dog's reward far more pleasurable than what he's missing out on by not coming. This is a situation in which it's virtually impossible to make too much of a fuss over your puppy's response.

You can begin training with the come command outside with just a short distance separating you from your dog. As you say, "Come," run backward a few steps and encourage your puppy to follow. If he does, even for a few steps, generously reward your puppy for his efforts with his favorite treats. As your terrier masters this important first step, increase the number of steps you take back before rewarding your puppy. This teaches him that he may have to come from a longer distance before receiving a reward.

If you have trouble with this and if, despite all your coaxing, your puppy still has a hard time putting two and two together, use a long *lead* (also called a *leash,* but I'm talking about one that's quite long) to help encourage your puppy and keep him from leaving the area. Put your puppy at the end of the lead and call your puppy to you. If he responds, reward him generously. If he ignores you, give a slight tug on the line and call your puppy again. Only tug the lead if your puppy ignores you and then gently reel him in, if necessary, to get the ball rolling. As your puppy makes the connection, use the lead less and less until your puppy is coming regularly without the leash reminders. Then remove the leash from the puppy and continue to work on the come command without the leash.

Staying in one place

The stay command not only comes in handy throughout the day, it can also help protect your terrier from danger. Because of their high energy levels, Jack Russells have a tendency to bolt out doors or across streets whenever something of interest catches their eyes. Rarely do they pay attention to cars coming their way.

The stay command is most easily taught with both vocal and hand commands.

1. **With your puppy sitting in front of you, place your open, flat hand in front of the puppy's nose and say, "Stay."**

2. **Take a few steps away (always beginning with your right foot) and then turn to face your dog.**

   Always step away from your puppy with your right foot when you want your dog to stay immobile. When you teach your puppy to heel, you will off with your left foot. This will indicate to your puppy that you want him to go forward. Don't confuse the two or you will invariably confuse your puppy, as well.

3. **If your puppy stays put, return to him, give him a treat, and say, "Okay."**

   Be sure to give him lots of praise for making such a good effort.

   If your puppy moves, go back into position and repeat the command.

REMEMBER

4. **Keep practicing until you can take 10 or 15 steps away while your dog stays put.**

Don't look your puppy directly in the eye when teaching him to stay. Some dogs take this as an aggressive stance on your part and may squirm, wiggle, or lie down to avert your stare. Instead, look over your puppy's head when giving the command.

WARNING

When your puppy has mastered the art of staying from quite a distance, you can make things a little more difficult. At a close distance (that you gradually increase), try jumping up and down or waving your arms to try to lure your puppy out of the stay command. If your terrier comes and tries to play with you, have him sit and stay and then try again. Your puppy needs to learn that he can't move off the stay command without your saying, "Okay." When your puppy won't respond to movement, try adding noise distractions. Yell, scream, talk, sing, do anything but say, "Okay." Gradually increase the distractions until you're sure your dog can sit and stay through almost anything.

Down and out

Like sitting, lying down is a natural act for your puppy. It's often easiest to catch your puppy in the act to begin this training. If you see your puppy position himself to lie down, give the down command and let him finish his action. If he continues as planned and lies down, praise him for being so perceptive.

TRY THIS

You can further this training by putting your puppy on a leash and placing him in a sitting position in front of you. Say the puppy's name to get his attention and then tell him, "Down!" Reach down and gently pull the puppy's front legs in front of him until he reaches a prone position (see Figure 8-1) and then give him lots of hugs and treats. When your puppy gets the general idea, you can switch to using a slight downward pressure between the puppy's shoulder blades to remind your puppy what's expected of him.

FIGURE 8-1:
Lying down is a natural act for your JRT.

© Kent and Donna Dannen/AKC Stock Images

TIP

Some dogs stiffen their bodies as you try to push them down. This can lead to a battle of wills and an unproductive training session. To address this problem, use an alternate method of asking your puppy to lie down.

1. **While kneeling at your puppy's side, say, "Down."**

2. **Reach across your puppy's shoulder with the hand nearest to the puppy and take a paw in each hand.**

3. **Using your elbow, gently press down on the puppy's back while using your hands to place the puppy's paws out in front of him.**

This combines both the placement of the paws and the downward pressure to encourage your puppy to lie down. If he even begins to relax downward, praise your puppy and show your pleasure. As your puppy starts to relax, he will accept this correction with greater ease and will soon lie down willingly.

4. **Reward him generously.**

REMEMBER

When giving a treat after the down command, it often is helpful to place the treat on the floor to encourage your puppy to stay in the down position when getting his treat. You also can scratch your puppy on top of his head or at the base of his tail, both of which can be accomplished while the dog is still down, to express your approval. The more comfortable your puppy is with the down position, the easier he will accept this training.

Heads and heels

Although stationary commands are great for calming your puppy down when he gets hyper and for keeping him from bouncing off the walls, there comes a time when you want to take your terrier with you and you need his cooperation. This is when the heel command comes in handy.

The proper position for heeling is with the puppy's neck even with your left leg. His front feet should stay even with yours, and he should look up at you every few strides to make sure he's in the proper position. This shows that your puppy is looking to you for direction and is trying hard to anticipate your next move. Occasionally saying, "Good dog" and giving a treat encourages your JRT to continue his actions.

TRY THIS

When your puppy has mastered the heel command and the sit command when stopping, practice making turns so that your puppy learns to follow you regardless of which way you're moving. Keep the turns simple at first and then progress to quicker turns that occur more often to keep your puppy's attention. You also can vary your pace to make things more interesting. All these techniques improve your terrier's responses and focus his attention on your next move. Soon he will be heeling on the leash like a pro.

REMEMBER

Remember that your puppy has never had to control his energies while on the move, and he's used to romping here and there as he moves about the house or yard. To teach your puppy to heel, you must first teach him that he has to pay attention to your movements and that he can move about on a leash without feeling unduly confined. Many puppies freeze when they realize there is something on them that will restrict their movement. They may lie down and refuse to move or may sit back against the leash, causing an unproductive tug-of-war. Other, more aggressive or curious puppies will run ahead of you and try to take you for a walk instead of the other way around. Either way, your puppy must learn that his job is to stay next to your leg, neither falling behind nor rushing ahead.

TIP

If your puppy is the reluctant type, use tidbits of food or small pieces of a doggy cracker to entice your puppy forward. Don't drag your puppy along in a mis-guided attempt to get him to follow you. You will only further ingrain in your puppy's brain that heeling is not a fun thing to do. Instead, use your puppy's desire for treats and his curiosity for what's in your hand to entice him forward. Praise him whenever he steps with you. At this stage, even a few steps forward should be praised because your puppy is working hard to overcome his fears and to trust your judgment. Be sure that the leash is somewhat slack and that your puppy truly is moving forward on his own accord. Remember to say, "Heel" each time you strike off, leading with your left foot. (You lead with your right foot when using the stay command.) Continue walking and praising until your puppy gains some confidence and is willing to walk forward without being timid.

REMEMBER

Keep your walking pace brisk. If you walk too slowly, your puppy will have too many opportunities to be distracted by the things around him. If you walk too fast, your terrier will have a hard time keeping up and will get frustrated. Walk as if you want to get somewhere and don't have time to dawdle.

When your puppy is heeling consistently, add the sit command each time you stop. This makes it easier to control your puppy or dog at intersections or when you see another dog approaching. Each and every time you stop, say, "Sit." Your terrier should remain at your left side and should sit even with your leg and with his front toes in line with your toes. If your puppy has a temporary lapse in mem-ory, bring his head up to look at you and then press him down on his haunches to remind him how to sit. Encourage your puppy to look at you while sitting so he knows when you're ready to move into the heel command again. You can do this by offering treats when your puppy performs correctly and by using your puppy's name before striking off.

TIP

After your puppy has mastered the basic heel on the leash, you can work toward heeling off the leash. Make sure you always have your leash close by in case your terrier has a lapse in concentration and starts to wander off.

THE TERRIER WHO TUGS

If your JRT has a bold streak, you may have a harder time holding him back than getting him to go forward. This is a puppy that needs to learn, first and foremost, that he has to pay attention to you regardless of the other interesting things going on around him. The easiest way to remedy this situation is to allow the puppy to train himself. How? It's really quite simple.

1. **Hold your puppy on a fairly short leash so there's not much extra slack between your hand and the puppy.**

   You should be holding the majority of the leash in your right hand, with your left hand picking up the slack between your right hand and your dog.

2. **Say, "Heel" and begin to walk forward, encouraging your puppy to walk with you.**

3. **If your puppy runs forward, simply stop.**

   Don't jerk the lead. This unnecessarily punishes your puppy. The mere act of stopping will effectively control the amount of leash your puppy has to work with, limiting his range of motion (see the figure). When your puppy reaches the end of his short leash, he will find that he can't go forward any farther and will turn back to look at you.

4. **After standing for several minutes, walk forward again.**

   Remember to lead with your left foot when you step forward.

(continued)

(continued)

5. If your puppy runs ahead again, stop and look at your puppy.

Repeat the process until your puppy figures out that running ahead will get him nowhere. He may want to pay a little more attention to you to see what you have in mind. Hint: Rewarding with treats when the lead is slack will speed up the process considerably!

At this stage, some puppies will decide that this is no fun and will jump and fight to try to gain their freedom. It is important that you not respond to these terrier temper tantrums. Instead, stand quietly, keeping the leash firmly in your hand, and wait for your puppy to stop fighting. When your puppy stops venting, bend down, pet him to reassure him, and then continue with your lesson.

Recognizing the Power of Praise

With all this schooling, teaching, and training going on, it's easy to forget to praise and reward your puppy with each and every correct response. Sometimes you can get so focused on expecting your terrier to do it right that you may forget that this kind of training is challenging for the puppy. Not only are you asking him to use a lot of concentration to focus on you, you're asking him to control his own natural energy to do what you want him to do. You're also asking him to repeat it several times. This is hard for a baby!

REMEMBER

Don't get so wrapped up in your lessons that you forget to praise and treat your puppy for good behavior. This is supposed to be fun for both of you, not a challenge to see how much you can teach your puppy in one day.

Consistency in each and every step of training is the key to success — consistency in your commands, consistency in your praises, and consistency in your corrections. It is unfair to correct your puppy one time for making a mistake and then let it go the next time it happens. This confuses the puppy and makes him wonder which way is really right. The same holds true for praise when the puppy responds correctly. If you praise him one time but not the next, and the response was the same both times, how does your puppy know whether he's responding correctly?

Nixing Negative Behavior

There may come a time during training that your JRT will decide there are far more interesting things to do than listen to you. You need to regain your puppy's attention, and you need a way to prevent his attention from wandering in the first place. By making yourself an important factor in your puppy's environment, he will learn to respect your wishes and will look to you for direction for his behavior. The following sections give you a couple of ways to accomplish this.

No — more than just a two-letter word

"No" is one of the most overused and misunderstood commands in dog training. More often than not, the puppy begins to think of the no command as part of his name rather than as a separate command. Many of these problems exist because either the word is screamed as the owner chases the dog through the house or the word is said so many times that it fails to sound like the original command. To your dog's ears, "No, no, no" sounds totally different than a firm "No." To further add to your puppy's confusion, "No" usually is used after the fact rather than before it. This leaves the puppy guessing as to what action caused your displeasure. Is it any wonder that terriers often ignore their owners?

TRY THIS

You can make the no command a bit more effective by using it to stop an action from occurring. It can be used when your puppy takes something that doesn't belong to him or when his attention wanders during a training session. If your puppy focuses his attention back on you, say, "Heel." If he responds correctly, give him a treat. The same technique can be used for a tempting tidbit or a toy on the ground. If you walk by a ball and your puppy starts to head toward it, say, "No." Give your puppy a treat and some praise when he responds by bringing his attention back to you.

Using diversionary tactics

There are times when you need to divert your puppy's attention. What do you do? As with children, you can use toys or noise to divert your puppy's attention away from the negative behavior and back to more positive things.

TIP

This technique can apply to anything from house-training to chewing on cords. A terrier is, by nature, rather obsessive. When he sets his mind on an action, he will continue to focus on that one thing until something else grabs his attention. This is where diversionary tactics come in very handy.

TRY THIS

Keep a can with a few coins in it within reach when relaxing in your home. If you see your puppy start to produce unwanted behaviors, either rattle the can or make a kissing noise to get his attention. Now you've created an opportunity to praise the puppy for an appropriate behavior.

You can use this technique with any number of inappropriate behaviors, from chewing on furniture to jumping on visitors. The idea is to divert your terrier's attention from the negative behavior so that he forgets what he was going to do. You then can praise your dog for his good judgment and for being so well behaved. This technique enables you to catch your puppy doing something right, such as deciding not to jump, instead of having to correct him for doing something wrong. It has the added benefit of keeping things positive, and it saves you from always feeling like the bad guy.

Creating a United Front

Perhaps the most challenging hurdles to overcome during puppy training are presented by children in the family. Like rambunctious puppies, children love to play and often will encourage your puppy into ill-mannered or destructive behavior because they think it's funny or cute. It is frustrating to spend hours teaching your puppy not to jump on people only to have your child encourage the puppy to jump on the couch! Not only is it frustrating to you, it also is frustrating to your puppy. Sometimes he's rewarded for jumping, and sometimes he's rewarded for *not* jumping — so which behavior is correct? You can see the dilemma.

TIP

Talk to your children before you begin your training. Explain to them the importance of keeping things consistent for your puppy. Involving them in your training lessons and obedience classes is a good way to help them understand the importance of consistency with your puppy's handling. Unless all involved parties are working together, training your puppy will take far more time and will be much more difficult that it would be otherwise. Trust me, training your JRT will be hard enough as it is. You don't need any outside factors making the training even more difficult.

Chapter **9**

Dealing with Behavioral Problems and Concerns

What do you do if your terrier is truly a terrorist and has a taste for even more destruction than normal, even for this breed? Don't worry too much yet. You can take steps to understand and minimize your terrier's destructive tendencies, and most JRTs can learn that some conduct just isn't acceptable.

REMEMBER

But you have to be understanding, as well. Some behaviors are just typically terrier, and no amount of training, punishment, or bribery will eliminate those habits. They are what they are, and you either learn to appreciate the good and the bad or drive yourself insane trying to undo what has taken nature over a hundred years to create.

Taming the Terrorist

What do you do if your dog simply refuses to obey your command or, worse, if he retaliates when forced to comply? There are several ways to manage defiance, and it is best to try different methods to find out which works best for your terrier.

Dogs in general have their own natural hierarchy within different packs and among different individual dogs. The hierarchy is determined by each dog's confidence, ability to fight, and ability to bluff. The dog who chooses to "roll over" first is usually ranked lower than the confronting dog. Rarely will a submissive dog confront or attack a more aggressive dog (one who is higher up in the pecking order). This occurs in wild dogs and coyotes as well as in domestic dogs, and it is useful to understand when training your puppy or dog.

Giving Time-outs

Like overactive children, Jack Russell Terriers often can become overstimulated, creating a hyper, difficult dog who literally ignores you even if you're right in front of him. The most common time for this behavior is when someone comes over to visit. Your JRT undoubtedly will be excited to see this new intruder, will all but maul your visitor to get attention, and will be jumping and barking in his excitement. Although this certainly is understandable in puppies, it is far less appealing in an older dog. At these times, you may need to employ the "time-out" method to get your terrier to settle down and come back to reality.

TIP

Ask people who are unfamiliar with your puppy or dog to ignore him until he has had time to settle down. You then can control the meeting if they are unacquainted, or you can allow your puppy to greet the visitor after he has calmed down enough to be manageable.

Time-outs can take several forms, depending on the terrier and his personality. Some dogs settle down simply by putting on a harness. Others need to be sent to a time-out corner to sit for a few minutes and think about their actions. Still others need to be sent to bed for a few minutes to settle down. Here's a rundown of each:

>> **Humbly harnessed:** Many JRTs love to put on a *harness* (a form of collar that goes around both the neck and rib cage, making it easier to lead an excited dog without choking him — see Figure 9-1) because it means they get to go somewhere; others see their harnesses as a means of confinement and become slightly intimidated. If your Jack Russell Terrier becomes even more wound up when you head for his harness, this is not the right time-out method for your puppy. If, however, your puppy becomes a bit subdued at the thought of being harnessed, this may be a good choice for your training.

TIP

REMEMBER

If possible, put the harness on your puppy just *before* your company arrives to set the scene for the next half-hour or so. This helps your terrier get into the right mindset for the upcoming visit, and it allows you to judge whether just wearing the harness is enough to temper your puppy's exuberance or whether you need to put him on a leash (which attaches to the harness) for a few minutes to tone down his energy level. When your company arrives, keep the puppy away from the door until your friends are safely inside. This prevents your puppy from getting so excited that he runs outside, creating yet another problem. Your visitors can pet the puppy for a few moments and then can ignore him after exchanging initial greetings.

After you set your puppy down, watch carefully to see that he doesn't jump on your guests. If he does, turn your back and reward him when he sits. By doing this several times — each and every time you expect company — your puppy will soon learn that he has to control his enthusiasm to enjoy the company of friends and family.

FIGURE 9-1:
Consider using a harness when training your JRT.

© Mark Hay

>> **The time-out corner:** The time-out corner is a corner of a room, usually the living room, where your dog gets to spend a few moments after he has ignored you or has done something wrong. Which corner you use really doesn't matter because the purpose is to get your puppy to sit still for several minutes to decrease his energy and anxiety level and to think about his behavior. Sometimes just getting the puppy to stop moving and to concentrate on sitting still is enough to get him to calm down.

For this method to be effective, it must be started when the puppy is old enough to control himself but young enough to make an impression. Use a tether to ensure that he stays in the corner. If he tries to move about, repeat the command and physically put the puppy back into the corner. Younger puppies should only be kept in the corner for a few minutes; older puppies can have longer time-outs to instill the impression that their actions were not appreciated.

Each and every time your puppy must be reprimanded, send him to his corner. At the beginning, you need to pick the puppy up and physically take him to the corner, making sure he doesn't cheat by moving away from the corner before being "released." Remember, though, to simply place your puppy in the corner without anger or aggression. Anger has no place in dog training, and your puppy will not understand if you're rough or angry. You will simply scare your young dog.

If your puppy stays in the corner without moving for a reasonable amount of time — say three minutes, to start — call your puppy onto your lap and pet him. As your puppy gets older, this time in the corner should increase to around ten minutes to be sure you have made an impression.

TIP

If your puppy moves during this time, send him back to the corner. After your puppy has been in the corner for the allotted time without coming away on his own, call your puppy over to your side or to your feet and have him lie down there for a few moments. This is used as a bridge command between the reprimand and full release. After the dog has been still for a few minutes at your feet, reach down, pet him, and let him go on his way.

As your puppy gets older, he will know from the tone of your voice and your actions when he's in trouble. Soon, your puppy will anticipate your actions by going to his corner whenever he senses that he needs to appease you. All it will take is a stern look from you, and your puppy will submissively head for the corner. Handling an impropriety with a stern word or look won't create resentment or hostility from your terrier. It's simply a way to portray your displeasure and to let your puppy know he has misbehaved.

Don't tempt your puppy with dangling cords and slippers left close to his play area. Puppies encounter enough temptations every day and have to work hard at being good. Remove obvious temptations (and those that aren't so obvious) from your puppy's reach to encourage success.

>> **Go to bed:** Another effective place to send a puppy for a time-out is to his bed, provided the bed is in a location where it's easily accessible and where you can keep an eye on your puppy when he's in the bed. Consistency will be the key.

When your puppy misbehaves, send him to bed in much the same way you as would send him to a corner by saying "Go to bed!" As with the corner, physically pick up the puppy and place him in his bed the first few times. Remain next to the puppy's bed to make sure he doesn't prematurely escape from his time-out and that he stays laying down and immobile. Your puppy will soon get the hint that this is the place to go when he's in trouble.

If you use the puppy's bed as his time-out place, remember that this is the puppy's own space. Don't ever physically intimidate a puppy or reprimand him in his own space. In other words, after you set the puppy in his bed, don't proceed to shake a finger and yell at him — and do not spank his bottom! These actions do nothing to emphasize your point and besides, this is the place the puppy can go to be "safe." You don't want the puppy to feel insecure in his "secure" place. Although you want the puppy to know he has done something wrong, you don't want him to be afraid of you and go running to the safest dark corner whenever you raise your voice.

>> **It's a crate thing:** Sometimes sending your puppy to a corner or to bed simply doesn't get the job done. These are the times when your terrier has gone past being able to listen to you and truly is on sensory overload. This can occur when the dog is in a new location for the first time in which there is an abundance of outside stimuli, or it can occur inside the home when several new things are going on at one time. In this situation, crating your puppy becomes the best and safest way to handle the behavior.

As with sending your puppy to bed, it is important not to view the crate as a place where you can exert your dominance over your puppy. Instead, use it as a safe haven for your puppy to calm down, to collect his thoughts, and to return his heartbeat to a normal level. Your puppy may not like being crated during these times. Most terriers will take offense at having their freedom taken away. It is important, however, to curb your puppy's natural excitement for his own good. When he is overly excited, your puppy may lose control over his physical functions or even work himself into a frenzy. Neither is good for your puppy. By allowing him to calm down for a brief period, your puppy will learn to regulate his excitement and will better be able to cope to new environments and stimuli.

If you see that your puppy is overstimulated, put a soft blanket in the crate and place your puppy inside. If possible, put the crate in a quiet corner where activity is at a minimum. You should only have to leave your puppy there for a short time (around 15 minutes) to get him to settle down — you'll know when the time is right because he will stop pacing and being anxious and will settle down in a corner or curl up and go to sleep. When this occurs, you can open the door and let your puppy out. Be sure to spend a few minutes talking and scratching your puppy when you let him out, but be careful not to rev him up again with too much enthusiastic praise.

REMEMBER

Don't let temper or ego enter into your terrier's training. Your puppy isn't purposefully going against your wishes; he's simply acting on impulses that interest him. Try not to take his indifference to your commands personally, but do make sure he knows you will get his attention, one way or another. Always do so, however, without resorting to violence.

Always remember to treat your Jack Russell with respect and kindness. This is your pet, and he relies on you for love and attention as well as for guidance. Although it is important for your terrier to know you're the top dog, it is just as important to show your puppy that you're fair and loving. You want to create a relationship with your dog that's free of intimidation and anxiety. Only by having a terrier that's comfortable in your presence will you fully gain your dog's cooperation.

Dealing with Digging Demons

Terriers dig. Period. They were bred to dig down to their quarry, and no amount of training will completely eliminate their natural instinct to explore the nether regions for rodents and prey. If you have a perfectly manicured lawn or garden and expect your terrier to never disturb a blade of grass or leaf of lettuce, you'll be sorely disappointed.

Instead of trying to train, beat, or coerce your dog into not digging, try to think of ways to allow your terrier to satisfy these natural urges without causing havoc to your landscaping. Usually, this means providing a time and a place where your terrier can dig to his heart's content without being scolded. This may be a corner of your yard or an area of an abandoned dirt parking lot. It doesn't matter where it is, it just matters that it's okay for your dog to dig there. You provide even more fun for your JRT by hiding doggy treats and biscuits under a few inches of dirt and then allowing your Russell to dig them up. By providing a place for your dog to "legally" dig and by visiting these digs several times a week, you can divert your dog's natural digging tendencies into a fun behavior.

If your safe digging spot is close by, take the time to train your dog to use it. If you see your dog digging in an area that's unacceptable, direct his attention to the acceptable area or simply pick him up and take him there. Tell him "Okay, dig." This will effectively turn digging into a command performance in which you control what's unearthed and where.

Chewing on This

All dogs chew, although their reasons for chewing change as they move from puppyhood to adulthood. They don't chew to frustrate you or to cause you grief. Instead, they chew to help their puppy teeth cut through their gums, to strengthen permanent teeth, and to clean their teeth and massage their gums. All dogs, and terriers in particular, use chewing as a type of pacifier to calm their nerves and to rid their systems of anxious energy.

REMEMBER

The negative side of chewing is that, without proper guidance and direction, your terrier literally can chew you out of house and home. The positive side of chewing is that you can provide acceptable chew toys for your terrier and can rid your dog of excess energy and damaging dental tartar all at once! Notice that I said *acceptable* chew toys. Not all of the toys, bones, and chewies you see at the local pet store are acceptable for your dog to gnaw on. Some are made of soft rubber and are for structured play, not continuous chewing. Others have pieces that may pose a choking hazard to your dog should he chew through the supporting structure. Because Jack Russell Terriers have notoriously strong jaws, choose your chew toys with caution and a great deal of care.

WARNING

Never give your terrier a bone that could break into small pieces or anything that is indigestible if swallowed. If the bone happens to break off with a sharp edge and your terrier ingests it, it could tear a hole in your dog's stomach or intestine and cause serious internal damage and even death. Likewise, indigestible material such as rubber or plastic may create an internal blockage leading to surgery or worse.

Perhaps the best chew toys available are the strong, nylon chew devices found on today's pet store shelves. These chew bones are made of strong, durable nylon and often come with a scent or a flavor added to make them more attractive to your terrier. Some are smooth and are shaped like knuckles or bones; others have raised bristles to help stimulate your dog's gums. These often are useful for dogs with a propensity for tartar buildup, though none is a good substitution for routine dental hygiene.

These toys provide excellent resistance for your dog's jaws and are crucial for jaw strength and health. They have the added benefit of being soft enough to prevent the wearing down of dental surfaces, but they are hard enough to provide a satisfying chew toy for your terrier.

Rope and floss chew toys provide the added benefit of "doggy dental floss" and can be used in conjunction with the harder nylon bones to complete your dog's dental regimen. The rope chew toys can get between your dog's teeth and literally can act as dental floss to clean the space between the teeth that harder chew bones can't reach. Because the rope and floss toys work with a gentle tugging that your dog naturally performs by himself, all you have to do is sit back and watch it work!

TIP

Provide a variety of chew devices for your dog and then stick with the ones he prefers the most. Although it is fine to leave the harder chew bones with your dog most of the time, rope chew toys can be easily shredded and ingested, so let your dog use those only under close supervision.

Barking Up a Storm

Barking is another aspect of canine behavior that's quite natural but can be quite annoying. Although you appreciate being notified of an intruder in your house, you don't appreciate being alerted to each and every passing car. Not only is excessive barking annoying to you, it will do nothing to endear you to your neighbors.

There is a big difference between a few warning barks to signal someone approaching the door and a half-hour barking jag that says your JRT is bored or irritated. Some JRTs also like to bark as a means of playing. Before you can be effective in changing your terrier's behavior, you need to determine the cause of your dog's barking. You then can choose the response most likely to succeed in that given situation.

Like most tempting first responses, yelling at your dog when he barks will not stop him from barking. Instead, your terrier will think you're joining in the fun and will bark longer and louder. In fact, he will enjoy barking even more because he thinks he has your approval and input!

TRY THIS

You need to teach your terrier that, although you appreciate the alarm for an approaching stranger, he must stop barking when commanded and must let you to deal with the person in peace. To begin the training, keep a leash handy so you can grab him as you head toward the door. As you approach the door, tell your dog "Enough!" in a firm, quiet voice and clip on the leash. If your dog barks after you have given the command, divert the dog's attention and give a treat for quiet. Take special care not to raise your voice and not to escalate your response in any way. You need to stay calm if you expect your dog to calm down.

TIP

If a leash is unavailable or if your dog is barking at an unknown sound or at you to get your attention, you can either ignore him or distract him. Don't pet or coddle a dog who's barking for attention. You will only create a spoiled dog who barks even more. If you can't ignore him, use the command "Enough!" again in a calm, commanding voice.

If you shake a can of coins or squirt a bit of water from a squirt bottle to distract your JRT, be sure not to telegraph your intentions with these devices. They work best when your dog thinks they occurred out of the blue and didn't come from you. This way, your terrier assumes that the correction was caused directly by the barking, not by your actions. You also can send your terrier to bed or to his time-out corner if he ignores your command to be quiet. After your terrier is quiet, praise him for being so cooperative.

The Chase Is On!

Terriers, by nature, love a good chase. After all, they were bred to hunt foxes and to chase them out of their dens. Like digging and barking, chasing cats, cars, children, and anything else that seems like a good sport are natural, inbred traits for your terrier and will prove to be particularly enticing.

Managing the chasing habit is especially important if your terrier likes to chase cars. For some unknown reason, Jack Russell Terriers have a particular penchant for anything with wheels and are almost obsessed with following these wheeled beasts. Unfortunately, the car can do a lot more damage to your terrier than your dog can inflict on the car.

The only way to correct this behavior is through leash training. Your dog must be made to respect your judgment. If your dog has been trained to respond to the command "No!" from Chapter 8, you will have a much easier time getting his attention away from the point of interest and firmly back on you — and then you can reward him for that attention. This takes consistent schooling and a lot of patience. When your dog can respond quickly and predictably on the leash, continue to work without the leash so that your dog's response will be both timely and consistent. This kind of schooling may get boring, but remember that it is very important. It may save your dog's life somewhere down the road.

To illustrate this point, one of my favorite terriers, Annie, was out with me at the ranch one day. I was giving a riding lesson to one of my students, and Annie was happily running here and there chasing squirrels and peering down holes. Suddenly, a coyote came out from of the woods, walked across the arena and proceeded up the hill. Annie took one look at the coyote, decided it looked like a good prey and took off running after the coyote. About 50 feet into the chase, the coyote decided to see what was pursuing it. Seeing the size of my little terrier and comparing her with his own mass, it decided that this tender little tidbit may make a great midday snack. I immediately yelled "Annie! No! Come!" and prayed that she would listen. Thanks to years of training and a strong respect for me, she stopped in her tracks and came running to me with the coyote not far behind. I was able to chase off the varmint and then thank my lucky stars that my training had paid off. I had my terrier in my arms to praise for her good behavior. Had I neglected this training, my dog may not be here today.

Managing Separation Anxiety

All dogs are social by nature, as proven by the formation of packs. When you separate your puppy from his littermates, you and your family effectively become his pack. When you have to be gone, whether for work or play, your puppy is left without his playmates. You can make this time easier for your puppy by doing the following:

>> Exercising the dog right before you leave the house

>> Leaving special chew toys for your puppy to use during your absence

>> Providing a quiet, peaceful area with food, water, and a soft bed for your puppy to enjoy while you're away

>> Keeping your departures and returns low-key and unemotional

>> Never punishing your JRT upon your return for any behaviors during your absence

Sometimes, regardless of your best efforts to provide a peaceful oasis for your puppy, he will still view your absence with some trepidation. You may find that your puppy barks for a few moments when left to his own devices but then settles into a quiet nap until you return. Or your puppy may get excited in the hopes of going with you but then, when he's convinced you're going out alone, resolve himself to playing solo until your return. In extreme examples, however, your dog may succumb to separation anxiety.

Dogs who truly suffer from separation anxiety exhibit classic signs of claustrophobia when left alone. Basically, they panic. In their efforts to calm their fears, these dogs may tear up carpet, try to claw their way through doors, or bark until they can't bark any more. Although puppies are natural demolition derbies and usually outgrow this destructive phase, an adult dog who suffers from separation anxiety is a different kettle of fish altogether.

You first need to understand why this behavior occurs. Because you have become your terrier's pack, he feels vulnerable when you're away. Essentially, his backup buddies have left him all alone. Instead of taking a deep breath and waiting it out as humans may do, your dog begins to fret about the fact that you may not return. The more he frets, the more anxious he gets. The more anxious he gets, the more he tries to escape the confines of the house to reunite himself with his pack. As his concern builds into panic, his actions escalate. He begins to claw at the carpet surrounding the doors or the screens covering the windows. He may lose control of his bodily functions and soil the carpet, or he may dig frantically at the door jamb to try to open the door. All these things can lead to significant destruction of property in a very short time.

REMEMBER

Separation anxiety is very real for your dog and is actually akin to a human anxiety attack or claustrophobia. Your dog isn't being destructive out of spite. He simply becomes so agitated that he can't control his anxiety.

REMEMBER

It's easy to become frustrated with an overly anxious dog, and your first instinct will be to punish the dog for his destructiveness. This probably is the worst course of action you can take. Imagine, for example, that your child gets separated from you in a grocery store. She calls out for you, but you're out of earshot. At first, your child isn't too concerned because you usually respond promptly to her calls for help. But as time passes and you don't reappear, your child gets more anxious. Pretty soon she's crying and then screaming, trying to find you. When at last you discover that your child isn't where you thought she was, you go searching and finally find her a few aisles away. Instead of consoling her frantic wails, you yell at your child and swat her on the behind for not staying close to you. What have you really taught your child? You've taught her that, not only is getting separated scary, it's even scarier when Mom shows up because then you're really in trouble. Now you've created a Catch-22. The child is anxious about getting separated and is equally anxious about the reunion.

By punishing your dog for his destructive behavior, you're teaching him to dread your departure and also to dread your arrival home, doubling your dog's anxiety level. The more anxious the dog is, the more destructive his behavior is. By punishing your dog after the fact, you're, in essence, creating a vicious cycle of escalating destructive behavior.

When faced with particularly troublesome behavior from your terrier, try to think like your dog thinks. Sometimes this can significantly change your perspective and can help you come up with more effective, nonpunitive ways of solving the problem.

The best way to diminish this problem is through safe confinement and constructive training. Remember the golden rule — never correct your dog after the fact. It simply has no meaning for your terrier and adds to his already-established anxiety level. Keeping this in mind, look at the following tips to help your terrier through this troubling behavior.

>> **Create the best environment possible for your dog while you're away.** Leave a radio on so that your terrier hears voices and doesn't feel quite so alone. Provide several toys and chewies that your dog can use to safely release his anxiety and rub your hands on them before you leave so they smell like you. Make sure the area is at a comfortable temperature and dim any glaring lights. By the same token, make sure your dog isn't left in total darkness, either.

>> **Decrease the attention you give to your dog before you leave the house.** If you always play and amuse him just before you go away, you've made separation that much harder. You inadvertently show your dog why he should miss you even more! Instead, quietly go about your business and, when it's time to leave, simply gather up your things and go. Don't say goodbye or tell him how much you'll miss him. Again, this may make you feel better, but it actually increases your dog's nervousness and anxiety.

>> **Acclimate your terrier to your necessary periods of absence by taking short walks away from home.** Make sure your dog has a doggy bed nearby and leave the house for an instant, stepping back in before your puppy has time to get worked up. Gradually increase the time in increments of just a few seconds. Avoid any drawn-out good-byes or threats about what you'd better find or not find when you get home. When you return, ignore your dog for the first several minutes, regardless of the condition of the house.

If some destruction has occurred, resist the temptation to begin yelling about how a dog can do so much damage in such a short amount of time. It won't make you feel any better, and it will nullify any benefit of this training session. If the dog has managed to resist his destructive impulses, you have good cause to praise him quietly. After you set the stage for a calm reunion, either praise your terrier for his good behavior or ask him to perform a simple obedience task such as sit or down. Then praise his cooperation.

Gradually increase the amount of time you're away until your dog gets the idea that you eventually will return and that your departure doesn't herald the end of the world. With a lot of practice and patience, you should be able to leave for a few hours without causing your dog to regress. Some dogs will permanently respond to this training; others will only stay calm for a few hours before giving in to their anxieties. If your dog falls into the latter category, confine your dog while you're away. This is less stressful for your dog, and it ensures that your house will remain intact. But if your dog has serious separation anxiety, crating the dog can make the behavior worse — your dog may injure himself! Try using doggie daycare or consulting with a behavioral specialist.

Dealing with Aggression

Some forms of aggression can be prevented; others seem to be inbred in the dog and controlling them could prove difficult. The best and easiest solution is to buy your Jack Russell Terrier from a reputable breeder who is known for having dogs with mild temperaments. Choose a puppy who had parents with a friendly nature and who doesn't consider himself the leader of the pack.

Aside from this obvious preventative first step, what can you do if your puppy seems to be getting rougher and rougher in his play or if you see signs of escalating aggressive behavior? The answer is to correct this behavior quickly and effectively before it gets out of control, and never lose your temper when you're dealing with a puppy with aggressive tendencies.

Puppy aggression

Tiny terrier teeth can do considerable damage to the flesh of your arms and hands. If you've ever had those little teeth sink into your finger instead of the sock you were holding, you don't need any convincing. Puppies naturally snarl, bite, and snap as they play with their littermates. Playing with you seems no different to them, and it's up to you to make your puppy see the distinction.

Although a rousing game of tug-of-war is good for everyone, it's important that you make sure your puppy knows roughhousing hurts. If your puppy puts your hand into his mouth, hold the puppy with your other hand, extricate your finger, and tell the puppy "No!" Stop playing with your puppy for several minutes to reinforce the point that nipping or mouthing human hands is unacceptable. After your puppy has calmed down for a few minutes, try playing with him again. Remember to correct your puppy each and every time he grabs too hard, and don't lose your temper no matter how much those little teeth hurt. The best way to prevent aggressiveness is by showing your puppy kindness. If he doesn't feel threatened by you, he won't be aggressive toward you.

REMEMBER

Correct your puppy by using understandable commands and by praising him for correct behavior. If you use physical punishment to correct a bad habit, you could be setting yourself up for aggression.

Dog-to-human aggression

Aggressive behavior in an older dog is a bit more difficult to deal with. It can manifest itself in several ways, including mounting, growling, and barking directly at a human. This is often caused by reprimanding a dog too harshly or by showing submission, thus encouraging more aggression. Keep in mind, however, that some JRTs growl just to growl. These dogs use growling more as a grumble than as a threat. Dogs who grumble at you seldom raise their hackles, bare their teeth, or show any other outward signs of aggression.

If you find your dog doing things such as barking at you for attention, grabbing a toy and running away before turning back and trying to entice you to play, or rubbing against you for attention, you have a dog who is displaying signs of dominance. Although this in itself may not turn into signs of aggression, it may very well eventually do just that. Then it will be up to you to solve the problem and to reassert your position as leader of the pack.

TRY THIS

One of the best ways to assert yourself without confrontation is to teach your terrier the basics listed in Chapter 8. This sets the ground rules in your dog's mind that there are commands he must obey. By gaining his cooperation in learning commands, you're teaching him that you are the head of the household.

TIP

These commands also prove useful in other areas and should be started immediately. While your dog is showing some aggressive traits, he should be schooled every day for at least a few minutes a day. Seriously dominant or fear-aggressive dogs exhibit behaviors such as raising their hackles and growling if you walk by. Don't try to confront your dog when he's doing this. If you find yourself getting into a battle of wills or if your dog growls at you when you try to move or position him, seek professional help. A truly aggressive dog can be dangerous to you and your family. Prompt attention to the problem from a professional who doesn't condone physical punishment is your best answer.

Don't stare at an aggressive dog. By looking such a dog in the eye, you're exhibiting a doggy signal for aggression. The dog may perceive this as a threat and retaliate. The best way to handle an aggressive dog is not through confrontation.

Some dogs show aggression only at feeding time or over a special toy or area. These terriers actually are protecting something that they feel is theirs, and they feel they must defend their prize from outside theft. Confrontation is not the way to handle this type of aggression. Instead, you need to let your terrier know that you're not there to steal his food or toy but that he must tolerate your presence to get a reward. You can do this by using training biscuits.

If you approach your dog's food bowl and he growls at you, call the dog over and show him a biscuit to get his attention. If he comes willingly, reward your terrier with one of the biscuits. You also can use cheese, pieces of hot dog, or any treat your dog has a taste for. The important thing is to be able to approach the toy or food without your dog feeling threatened. By making your presence even more rewarding, your dog may look forward to having you around and not be so inclined to chase you off.

Food guarding and possession aggression aren't usually easy to resolve, however, and can be dangerous threats to children. Seek professional help if rewarding your dog for appropriate behavior isn't resolving the problem.

Dog-to-dog aggression

Some terriers aren't aggressive with their owners but are extremely aggressive with other dogs. I'm not talking about a dog who runs up to anything and everything wagging his tail or wanting to play. I'm talking about a Jack Russell Terrier who wants to eat every other living, breathing dog, regardless of size. Not only can this be frustrating when trying to socialize your terrier, it also can be downright dangerous if the dog that your terrier chooses to attack is ten times his size.

Early socialization through park play and obedience classes is the best solution for this type of aggressiveness. If your puppy is introduced to other dogs and learns the social ins and outs of doggy behavior, he is less likely to turn aggressive. Because some of the puppies he meets will be more aggressive and some will be more timid, your puppy will learn to judge the other dogs' reactions and to act accordingly. Sometimes he will win and sometimes he will back down. This interaction will usually lead to acceptable behavior.

If, despite your efforts at socialization, you find your terrier in the middle of a dog fight, don't reach down in the middle of it to try to stop your dog. This is a good way to get bitten! Instead, create a diversion by spraying the dogs with water from a squirt bottle or by causing another distraction. Remember that the fighting dogs are focusing 100 percent on their disagreement and aren't likely to notice you're nearby. A dog in this situation has little respect for human hands or feet and is likely to mistake your limbs for those of his opponent.

TRY THIS

The best course of action is to control your terrier in the first place by keeping him firmly on a leash until you're sure of his reaction to the other doggy players. Only after you've assured yourself that everyone will get along should turn your terrier loose. Keep a close eye on him for a few minutes to satisfy yourself that your judgment was correct. By keeping your dog on a leash at the beginning, you can easily remove your dog from harm's way if another dog begins to look aggressive.

4

Creating a Healthy Lifestyle

Although playing, exercising, and frolicking with your Jack Russell are by far the most fun parts of JRT ownership, with this fun comes responsibility. This includes caring for your terrier's health and well-being through proper diet, exercise, and veterinary care throughout its various life stages. This part guides you through the confusing and often daunting morass of health routines, problems, and concerns most important to your JRT's well-being. It also explains some of the medical symptoms and disorders that you may encounter and gives you solid information about healthy diets for your Jack Russell.

Although training is undeniably important, it's even more important to have fun with your Jack Russell Terrier. After all, that's why you bought a dog in the first place, isn't it? And having fun with your terrier doesn't have to be limited to playing ball or going for a walk. When you think about it, the possibilities truly are endless. This part helps focus your efforts on activities that fit within your lifestyle. From having fun at the beach to Jack Russell Terrier trials to trips to faraway places, this part helps get you on your way and helps make your planned outing a successful one. It may even prompt you and your family to take up a new pastime.

Finally, this part addresses special concerns for your JRT, including the difficult dilemma of saying good-bye to an older friend.

IN THIS CHAPTER

» **Finding a great vet**

» **Knowing how to handle an emergency**

» **Getting shots for your Jack Russell**

» **Getting a handle on pests**

» **Deciding whether to breed your JRT**

Chapter **10**

Keeping Your JRT Safe and Sound

N ot all veterinarians are created equal. Depending on where you live, you may have many veterinarians available to you or only a few to choose from. You would be wise to check out several before deciding which vet is for you and your terrier. Some veterinarians have a distinctly negative opinion of JRTs based on previous encounters. This may not be in your best interest. This chapter will help guide you through the selection of a veterinarian for your Jack Russell, and it will give you some solid questions to ask your vet to make sure your terrier remains happy and healthy.

Doctor Jekyll or Mr. Hyde?

Exert the same care in selecting a veterinarian for your dog as you would in selecting a doctor for yourself and your family. Ridiculous? Not in the least. After all, your dog is part of the family, isn't he? What do you look for in your personal physician? Experience, compassion, dependability, ability to communicate with you, closeness to home, compatible dog-care philosophies, and so on. All these factors are important, as is knowing that your doctor keeps up on new medical developments, medications, and treatments.

In addition to the preceding, you want to be sure that

>> The office has overnight facilities, in case your dog needs to stay there a day or two for observation or for treatment.

>> The facilities are clean.

>> You're comfortable with the way the clinic staff handles the animals.

>> Food and water are fresh and available.

>> The doctor's fees are within your budget.

An older, more established veterinarian may charge more than a young vet just starting out. Some younger veterinarians are willing to charge less in order to establish a practice. Don't overlook the opportunity to utilize a fresh eye to the field of veterinary science just because of a person's age. Many young vets are more compassionate than their older counterparts because they haven't been hardened by experience, and they may bring to your relationship a broader knowledge of current veterinary medicine.

TIP

A crate is a useful tool for transporting your dog to and from the vet's office. Place his favorite blanket and toy inside to minimize the trauma of a visit to the vet. Remember, however, that your dog also should be able to associate the crate with pleasurable and fun car rides such as trips to the beach.

Judging bedside manners

Rapport with your vet is important. You need to be able to communicate well with him when explaining your terrier's symptoms and actions when he's ill, and you want to feel comfortable that the veterinarian will explain your dog's condition without being condescending or impatient. Also, does the vet return your calls promptly? It sounds like an obvious question, but all too often the answer is no. When you're nursing a sick dog, a timely call-back from your vet is as appreciated as your pediatrician's response time when you're a first-time mother with a sick baby who can't tell you what hurts! Remember, your dog is part of the family, and he deserves your vet's best care and attention.

In truth, you and your vet should have as good a rapport as you and your personal physician have. Knowing what to expect from the beginning avoids unpleasantness and ill feelings in the long run. Your vet may assume you know all the ramifications of his diagnosis. If there is any question in your mind, ask additional questions of your vet. Don't leave your vet's office until you're confident you understand everything that is recommended and exactly what effort and costs those recommendations entail.

Understanding vet's fees

It is important that you understand the charges for specific procedures and treatments before you agree to the treatment so that, when the bill arrives, you're prepared and won't have to obtain a second mortgage on your home. This also enables you to make an educated decision whether to proceed with a given treatment. When taking your dog in for a yearly physical, for example, will you be charged just for a physical or, as is often the case for older dogs, will special tests be required? If these tests determine that there is a problem, will you have the money to invest in additional treatment? How extensive will that treatment be? Will this be a one-time event? Or will it entail ongoing costs and treatment? As you can see, some early research will help you make a good decision at the start.

TIP

Ask whether your vet is accustomed to working specifically with Jack Russell Terriers. If so, he is more likely to understand and effectively treat inherent health problems specific to the breed (see Chapter 15). Moreover, a vet familiar with JRTs may have more patience with a rambunctious dog. But be wary of a vet who assumes that all JRTs are problematic. The vet may not give your dog the conscientious attention and observation he deserves.

The Lowdown on Shots

Veterinary medicine has come a long way, and you can now order vaccinations for almost every modern dog disease. It's incumbent upon you as a responsible JRT owner to make sure your terrier is immunized against diseases that often can be fatal. It would be a tragedy to lose your pet due to a lack of simple preventive medicine.

Some of the diseases currently preventable through vaccination include rabies, distemper, leptospirosis, canine hepatitis, kennel cough, Lyme disease, and coronavirus. As your JRT gets older, other shots will be required. Ask your vet whether he sends out shot reminders to keep you abreast of your JRT's vaccination schedule.

When you first get a puppy or dog, one of your first calls should be to your vet. You should tell him what shots your Jack Russell already has had and should ask him which shots are still needed and when. Vaccination recommendations vary from area to area and from vet to vet. The following provides a brief summary of the most common vaccinations recommended and when they usually are administered:

>> At birth, puppies obtain a certain amount of immunity to disease through their dam if she herself has been immunized. This immunity, however, lasts only for a few weeks.

>> At six to eight weeks, your puppy will require vaccinations for canine distemper, infectious hepatitis, parainfluenza (CPI), canine adenovirus type 2, coronavirus, and parvovirus.

>> Puppies should be revaccinated every two to three weeks until 16 weeks of age.

>> At around 12 weeks of age, your puppy also should receive a leptospirosis shot and, if recommended by your vet, a Lyme disease vaccine.

>> Many veterinarians wait until the puppy is 1 year old to administer the first rabies shot; others give the first shot at 14 to 16 weeks.

Check with your vet for his recommendation because it may differ from those listed here. Boosters for all vaccinations are often given annually.

Managing Bumps and Bruises

With a dog as active as a JRT, injuries are difficult to avoid. A bit of knowledge as to what to do when one occurs can save your dog's life or, at the very least, can reduce his discomfort until you can get him to the vet. The following discusses some specific problems you may encounter and how to handle them if they do occur.

>> **Bleeding:** If your dog sustains an open wound that is bleeding profusely, control the bleeding immediately by covering the wound with a clean towel or cloth. Apply gentle pressure, adding additional coverings as necessary. Elevate the wound and use a cold pack, continuing to apply pressure to the wound. In case of a chest wound, place a piece of plastic over the wound, securing him to make it as air tight as possible. As soon as you notice such an injury, get your terrier to a vet as quickly as possible.

>> **Eye injuries:** If your dog's eye comes into contact with an irritant, wash the affected eye with plenty of water. You can do this by using an ear bulb or a plastic syringe. Be careful that you keep the stream of water or saline gentle so as not to cause further damage. If your dog's eye has been punctured or lacerated, wrap the dog in a warm blanket and take him to a vet right away.

>> **Injured limbs:** Digging is one of the Jack Russell's inbred traits. Sprains or fractures can occur as a result of excessive, spirited digging. If your dog comes in limping and looks to be in pain, keep your dog warm and quiet, try to steady the injured limb with a support bandage without pulling or tugging on it, and take your pet to your vet. A mild analgesic will often help.

REMEMBER

Because of the Jack Russell Terrier's intense love of digging, one of his most common injuries is a torn or removed toenail. If you notice that your JRT is limping or lying down licking his paw, check to see whether he has damaged one of his toenails. If he's limping badly, call your vet.

Active dogs who share their lives with horses are apt to be kicked or stomped on occasionally. If this happens, avoid unnecessarily moving your dog and seek attention if the injury appears to be severe.

>> **Snake bites:** In the case of a snake bite, try to keep your dog as quiet as possible, keep him warm and, if you're unable to contact your vet immediately, apply pressure between the dog's heart and the bite. Symptoms of snake bite include nausea, listlessness, and swelling at the site. Fang marks often are apparent. If you know the snake was venomous, get your JRT to a vet immediately. Snake bites can be fatal.

>> **Electric shocks:** JRT's love to chase and bite everything. If your dog gets hold of an electric cord or conduit and bites through it, use a plastic or wooden stick to move the cord away from your pet, look for burn signs inside his mouth, keep the dog warm, and rush him to a vet. Many times, the injuries caused by electrocution aren't readily apparent, so you should act quickly and get your Jack Russell immediate medical attention.

WARNING

You can receive a shock yourself by touching a dog who has been electrocuted. Protect yourself by removing the cord from the socket or by pushing your JRT away from the electrical source before attempting to handle him.

REMEMBER

Keep in mind that a dog in pain may bite, even if he is normally very friendly. Use caution when handling your injured dog.

Knowing When You Have an Emergency

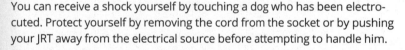

Keep your veterinarian's phone number handy so you can quickly access it in case of an emergency. Emergencies come in many forms and, no matter how careful you are, they can and do occur. Jack Russell Terriers are such active little critters that a thorn deeply imbedded in a paw or a laceration from chasing a ground squirrel isn't uncommon. Unless you're paying close attention to your JRT's actions, you may not notice these injuries until they become infected or until your terrier becomes noticeably lame. If you're familiar with the Jack Russell's busy nature, you know that this may be days after the fact.

Give prompt attention to any signs of bleeding or infection, along with difficulty in breathing, limping, convulsions, excessive drooling, listlessness, inability to urinate, vomiting, swelling, or fever. Symptoms can vary widely and can be signs of problems ranging from poisoning to a bee sting to hypothermia. If you aren't sure what's wrong with your terrier and he appears to be "not quite himself," a quick call or visit to the vet is warranted. He or she can tell you whether further treatment is necessary. Some external emergencies are obvious (open wounds, cuts, bruises, slivers in paws, or foreign objects in ears), but many are internal and only can determined and treated by your veterinarian.

WARNING

Call the vet and remove the collar on your JRT if you notice that your terrier's breathing is labored, very rapid, shallow, loud, irregular, or if he gasps for air, displays a blue tongue, or loses consciousness. These symptoms suggest a respiratory problem that could be fatal.

Taking your dog's temperature

So that you can be prepared to answer your vet's questions, check to see that breathing passages are free of obstructions, write down any symptoms you have been noticing, and take your dog's temperature. To take your JRT's temperature, lubricate and insert a rectal thermometer (preferably digital) into your dog's anus about 1½ inches deep and leave it for one minute. Hold your terrier still and standing during this time. (You do not want him to sit on the thermometer!) A JRT's natural temperature ranges from 100° to 102°F.

If your vet asks you to check your dog's pulse, lay your dog down on his side. Place your hand on the femoral artery, which is located where the thigh meets the abdomen on the back leg. Count the pulse rate for one minute. A normal pulse is 80 to 100 beats per minute while resting.

Leaving some things to the pros

Some types of treatment are best administered by a licensed vet, and you can cause more problems for your terrier by taking matters into your own hands.

>> Don't try to remove a splinter or other object that appears to be deeply imbedded.

>> Don't try to straighten a limb that may be broken.

>> Don't try to induce vomiting if you suspect your dog has ingested a toxic or poisonous substance unless specifically directed to do so by your vet's office. Many poisons are more dangerous if regurgitated and can cause additional danger to your JRT if vomiting is induced.

REMEMBER

KNOWING YOUR TERRIER'S TYPICAL READINGS

During one of your routine visits to your vet or at home, on your own, find out what temperature and pulse rate are normal for your individual JRT. Write this information down and keep it in a safe place so that you can compare it to the readings you get down the road, should you suspect that something is amiss with your terrier. Your vet will find this information useful when diagnosing whether the readings you're giving him are abnormal for your individual JRT. He or she sees hundreds of dogs a month and is not likely to remember the specifics for your dog without a reminder.

REMEMBER

If your dog has been hit by a car or has suffered an extreme trauma, immobilize him and get him to the vet immediately. Wrap your dog in a blanket to keep him warm and place him in a small crate or on a board to keep him totally immobilized. Talk to your JRT and do all you can to comfort him on the way there to try to keep him shock and trauma to a minimum. Your presence and your voice can be very soothing to your Jack Russell in times of trauma; the more you do to keep him calm, the better you will both handle the situation. Keep your own actions and demeanor calm so that your JRT doesn't sense your emotional distress, which would cause him additional anxiety.

WARNING

Your vet may request that after a trauma to body or limb, you keep your JRT subdued and avoid excessive activity. If you know JRTs at all, you will know how ridiculous this request is. Your best bet for a day or two after such a trauma is to use a crate — the only method short of drugging your dog that keeps him calm, cool, and collected.

Keeping Out Those Nasty Pests

As if dealing with summer mosquitoes, ants, and spiders around the house isn't enough, having a dog around creates a whole new environment for a different set of creepy crawlies. By paying attention to these little invaders before they become a problem, however, you can save your Jack Russell and yourself significant discomfort and frustration.

The JRT flea circus

Spring is the season when thoughts usually turn to planting a garden, spring cleaning, and summer vacation plans. It also harkens the arrival of fleas, those teeny little pests that can make your dog's life miserable. Fleas are well adapted to survive, and an adult female flea can lay up to 50 eggs a day on your dog. Soon, these eggs fall off the dog's hair onto your bed, carpets, and upholstery. After hatching, the eggs develop into tiny larvae and feed primarily on adult flea feces that accumulate in pet areas along with the eggs. This is not a very appetizing prospect, but it's one that reinforces the importance of ridding yourself not only of the fleas on your dog but also those both inside and outside of your home.

TIP

Kill fleas both indoors and outdoors and make sure you're using a flea treatment that's both safe and effective. Many flea treatments contain chemicals that can be harmful to you, your dog, and your children. Opt for natural remedies, such as cedar shampoos and fine-toothed flea combs, instead.

WARNING

Most flea sprays, shampoos, and powders aren't advisable for use on a pregnant or nursing dog or on very young puppies, unless otherwise directed by your vet. Also, special preparations are available for homes with pregnant or lactating women, infants, or young children.

REMEMBER

Does your dog scratch or chew his backside, chest, or genital area? Does he sport bald and reddened spots? If so, there's a good chance those nasty little bugs are lurking among your terrier's hair. You shouldn't assume that, because you can't see them, they aren't there. Only combing your dog's hair with a fine-toothed flea comb or giving him a bath with a good flea shampoo will verify whether they're present. (And keep in mind that the presence of a single flea can cause a reaction in a flea-allergic dog.)

Fighting fleas must be done on several fronts. First, determine how extensive a flea problem you have. Have dogs or cats lived in your home prior to your moving in with your terrier? Or is your pet the first one in the residence? In the former case, you may have an entrenched flea problem that requires treating not only your pet but also the rugs and upholstery. If the latter is true, it will be your job to keep these nasty little biters from ever taking up residence.

Only about ten percent of fleas in a house reside on a dog, so you need to pay special attention to the carpets inside and the yards around your house. You can treat carpets by sprinkling Borax — or any of the other products currently available on the market — on your carpet and then vacuuming thoroughly. Make sure you seal the collection bag and dispose of it outside your home. Because fleas require humidity to survive and Borax dehydrates them, it's a great flea treatment and, to my knowledge, is safe for both you and your carpet.

If the flea infestation is severe, you may consider a flea bomb or, in the worst scenarios, having a professional treat the house. If you choose all-out warfare, make sure all items on the floor are removed, put away, or covered and be sure to thoroughly ventilate the area afterward. Because these methods often use toxic substances, only use them as a last resort and take care to protect any surface that may be used for food at a later time. Move your family and your pets out before flea bombing.

Your veterinarian is an excellent source of information for products available that are both effective and safe for you and your dog. Keep in mind that professional rug cleaning does not rid your carpets of fleas unless a solution is included in the cleaning process that specifically kills fleas. Also remember that there are fleas outside your home as well, and the same care should be taken to rid your yard and the surrounding area of fleas and their friends. Although fleas don't carry severe diseases, they do account for more than half of doggie dermatological problems and can cause similar problems in humans.

Fleas that actually reside on your pet can be difficult to eliminate. Your veterinarian may suggest one of several products on the market that safely kills fleas and prevents them from propagating. Feed-through products (which are sprinkled on your dog's food and then ingested) work well, are easy to administer, and pose fewer health risks than a topical treatment may. Spot-on topical treatments also may work for your JRT and carry a lower risk than some other flea products. Flea collars have produced mixed results, and some may even be harmful to your terrier. Check with your vet before strapping one on.

Natural remedies such as feeding your dog garlic and brewer's yeast also may work to rid you and your terrier of these pests. Many people swear by them, although few tests prove the efficacy of these food supplements. If you want to try it, go ahead. It won't harm your JRT and it may work for your pet.

Tick, tack, oh no!

Fleas aren't the only pests that threaten your Jack Russell. Ticks also can be a problem, though they are more common in wooded or rural areas than in the city. Ticks are somewhat easier to manage than fleas because they don't infest the inside of your house, but they do carry more serious diseases. Check your JRT for ticks immediately after he has been out playing in the woods. Ticks can carry Lyme disease, Babesia, tick paralysis, tick fever, or Rocky Mountain spotted fever, all of which are potentially fatal for your terrier and also can make humans quite sick.

Ticks are small, round, and are found anywhere on your dog's body, but most commonly around his ears, neck, head, and feet. They cling to one spot, insert their heads into your dog, and feed on his blood. One easy way to remove them is by using a pair of tweezers and pulling firmly but gently away from your dog's skin. Usually, the tick will detach in its entirety, although occasionally the head will stay in your Jack Russell — remove the head if you can to prevent infection of the site. If signs of an infection develop, take your JRT to the veterinarian immediately. If possible, drop the tick in alcohol to kill it. If alcohol is unavailable, find a rock and smash the tick to kill it.

SKINNED ALIVE!

Many skin irritations are the result of insect or flea bites that cause your dog to scratch himself, thus aggravating the problem. Flea allergies are caused by the saliva in the flea's bite and can cause your dog to be miserable for days, especially if he hasn't been exposed to fleas for some time. Don't automatically assume, however, that your JRT's itching fits are caused by fleas. Dry skin also can be a common but less-serious cause of skin irritation, and it is often easily treated using topical treatments or special conditioning shampoos.

In addition, some skin irritations are the result of allergies to food, pollen, dust mites, or mold. Symptoms include scratching, biting, chewing, and constant licking. Treatments vary widely from cool baths to allergy shots or steroids that reduce inflammation (if present), depending on the type of skin irritation and his cause. Corticosteroids aren't recommended because they can have negative side effects and should be considered only as a last resort.

WARNING

Don't try to burn a tick with a match or use petroleum products such as gas or kerosene. These "remedies" could put both you and your Jack Russell in danger. Alcohol, on the other hand, is quite safe if you apply it only on the tick and not on the surrounding skin area. Be sure to wear gloves and to avoid contact with the ticks' body fluids to avoid infecting yourself. Make sure to thoroughly wash your hands with hot soapy water after removing it.

Ticks thrive in long grass near wooded locations. If you have a heavy tick infestation in your area and your dog spends a great deal of time outdoors, keep the grass mowed and the weeds down to reduce areas where ticks can hide. Make a habit out of checking your terrier regularly for these little bloodsuckers. The sooner they're removed, the less discomfort they will cause your JRT.

Watch out for the creepy crawlies

Internal parasites include hookworms, whipworms, ascarids, threadworms, heartworms, lungworms, and tapeworms. These and other unsavory creatures are a real threat to your dog's health. Most puppies are infected at birth, through their dam, with some type of worm. It is important to develop a vet-supervised worming schedule right from the start.

Worms, especially heartworm, can cause serious health problems, which is why a regular worming schedule is important. Like any other health maintenance program, however, it shouldn't be administered willy-nilly. Your veterinarian is the best person to advise you if and when your terrier needs to be wormed. Usually he will ask you to bring in a stool sample for testing. From the results of that test, he or she will prescribe a wormer based on your JRT's individual needs.

OPEN WIDE!

The time may come when you need to open your dog's mouth to administer medication. To open your dog's mouth successfully, first practice without intending to insert any medication — and using plenty of treats. After your JRT is comfortable having his mouth handled, you can begin.

Put your hand across his muzzle, grasp gently, say "Open!" as you push a thumb on his lip behind his canine tooth and lift his upper jaw.

- **Pill poppin':** If you're administering a tablet or a capsule, first give your JRT and piece of cheese (to get him used to the flavor). Gently push it all the way to the back of your terrier's throat and place it in the center of your JRT's tongue (see the figure above).

  If your Jack Russell is particularly skilled in evasion tactics, it often helps to wet the tablet or capsule or to wrap it in a soft food your dog enjoys (such as cream cheese or a piece of hot dog) to help it go down more smoothly. Otherwise, you may find the pill laying on the carpet in the next room and your crafty JRT applauding himself at his ingenuity. Remember to give your terrier a treat after each successful attempt and to use slow, gentle movements to avoid startling or frightening your terrier.

- **Liquid medication:** In the case of liquid medication, slowly tilt your dog's head back and hold his muzzle shut by putting your hand around it. Using a medication syringe, work the plastic tip into the back corner of the mouth. Give the medication slowly enough so that it won't choke the dog or leak out through the corners of his mouth. Never give your Jack Russell medication meant for humans or anything that hasn't been prescribed by the vet. These remedies can be unsuitable and dangerous to your dog. If you must administer foul-tasting medication, you may be in for a bit of a struggle. Most dogs don't like to have their mouthes handled and will probably try to spit the ugly stuff out. As I always say, though, better a petulant dog than a sick one!

Every dog should be on a heartworm prevention medication during warm months.

Contact your vet if you notice your dog scooting his rear end on the ground or if you see any other behavior that seems odd or indicates that your dog has an itchy rear end. This may be a skin-related problem, impacted anal sacs, or it may indicate worms. In any event, have a medical professional examine your dog. If you notice a white stringy substance or blood in your JRT's stools, contact your vet and take in a sample for evaluation.

Resist the impulse to purchase over-the-counter worming medications for your puppy. These treatments aren't as effective as those prescribed by your vet, and they can often even be dangerous to your puppy's health if given without prior parasite testing.

Jack Rabbits or Jack Russells?

Unless you plan to become a professional, responsible breeder, don't decide at your dog's first heat that having a litter of puppies is a neat idea. Breeders choose their brood-stock with rigorous guidelines and an eagle eye. Unless you've chosen as your pet a superior JRT specimen and have bred dogs before, you're getting in way over your head. Deciding to breed your JRT could produce litters of inferior-quality puppies, create an influx of displaced dogs, put your family pet in jeopardy, and ultimately lead to more euthanized Jack Russells.

Don't breed your dog because you feel that the process will be a good experience for your children to see the wonders of nature. Rent a video, instead!

Jack Russell Terriers are cute but they aren't for everyone and aren't as portrayed on TV programs or movies. Witness the number of JRTs who end up in rescue organizations and animal shelters. Your female dog isn't a source of funding for your family's next trip. Don't allow well-meaning friends to convince you that, because they would "love to have one of Spate's puppies," you should oblige by providing litters of them.

Breeding is for pros

Dog breeding is serious business. Unfortunately, the popularity of the breed has caused many people to purchase female Jack Russells for the sole purpose of breeding them and earning a few bucks on the side. This is not what a responsible breeding program is about. Breeders rarely make a fortune on their litters because there are many costs that defray any profit that could be made. Puppies must have their tails docked, their dewclaws removed, and their early shots provided. Breeding females must be routinely examined to ensure their health, and complications during the birthing process aren't uncommon. Moreover, the original cost of breeding stock is significantly higher than that of a pet-quality animal, not to mention the cost of the stud fee to breed with a quality sire.

The benefits of spaying or neutering

There are many advantages to spaying your female dog or neutering your male dog. In males, neutering reduces problem behaviors such as fighting, aggression, territorial marking, and mounting. It also reduces the incidence of prostate problems and eliminates the possibility of testicular cancer. In females, spaying prevents the need for *diapering* (the use of a plastic diaper and pad to collect the bleeding that occurs during estrus) during heat cycles, unwanted litters, and the considerable nuisance of having unwelcome males camp on your doorstep or against your fence like fawning Casanovas. It also can help prevent *pyometra*, a serious and potentially fatal uterus infection, and greatly reduces the likelihood of your Jack Russell developing mammary cancer later in life.

If you own male and female Jack Russell Terriers, spaying and neutering eliminates the necessity for keeping your dogs separated every time the females are into heat (four to six weeks at a time, twice yearly). Many a backdoor screen has been shredded by the attentions of a male trying to get to his mate. Dogs also have been known to jump fences and to dig holes the size of the Grand Canyon to reach the object of their affections. An intact male Jack Russell kept away from a female in heat truly is a miserable animal, and he will do virtually anything to satisfy his natural urge to procreate.

Neutering, when performed by a competent vet, is relatively safe and painless. In some areas, license fees for neutered dogs are reduced, thus paying for the neutering procedure in the long run.

Neutered dogs are happier and are less apt to seek ways to roam the neighborhood. They are less aggressive and are less likely to be the object of aggression than their intact counterparts. They also are less likely to try to mate with the neighbor's Pit Bull or Rottweiler. As a result, risks of injuries are lessened, saving you expensive vet bills. Neutered males are more laid back, are better behaved, and make for a more contented pet. Because their natural urges are diminished, their anxiety level is lessened, as is their propensity for destructive behavior.

Chapter **11**

Feeding Your JRT

Your responsibility as a pet owner is to supply your Jack Russell with the best nutrition possible, just as you do for your family. Don't base your choice of dog food on price alone. The fact that a particular brand is on sale shouldn't be the determining factor. Carefully check the listed ingredients. After you find a brand that meets your terrier's nutritional requirements and that your JRT seems to like, stick with it.

Dogs aren't like people; they don't require variety in their diet. In fact, frequent changes in food are likely to upset your dog's stomach and cause intestinal distress every time you switch brands. Some dogs may appear to like the new dog food at first but then become bored with it, so there is something to be said about buying new dog food in small quantities. This way, you won't waste your money and get stuck with a 50-pound bag of dog food that your finicky Jack won't touch.

Finding the Right Food for Your JRT

You're usually safe buying a well-known, high-quality dog food that has undergone rigorous feeding trials and that meets the Association of American Feed Control Officials (AAFCO) recommendations. If you're still lost among the morass of available choices, check with your veterinarian for a recommended brand that will meet your JRT's needs. The lamb and rice varieties may prevent skin irritations that the varieties containing corn may cause, so consider this option if your dog seems to get hot spots or has itchy skin.

DRY, CANNED, OR SEMIMOIST?

The following list highlights the pros and cons of dry, canned, and semimoist dog food.

- Dry food, while less appealing to your Jack Russell, is most convenient and is the preferred dog food choice. The hard nuggets give your JRT's teeth a subtle cleaning as she eats, and the texture forces your dog to work a little at her meal. This provides the "crunch resistance" that your terrier needs for strong teeth and jaws.

- Canned food is more expensive, has a higher moisture content, and often contains color enhancers and sugar that your JRT doesn't need. Because it offers no fiber substance, its prolonged use can cause plaque on your dog's teeth. It also lacks the hard texture your terrier needs to develop normal chewing action and good teeth. If your JRT is on a canned-food-only diet, supplement your dog's diet with plenty of chew sticks, rawhide bones, and dog biscuits so that these needs can be met in other ways.

- Semimoist food tastes good and is handy, especially when you travel with your dog. It's high in sugar content, however, and is the least favored as a nutritional choice. It offers so little resistance that it provides no strengthening value to your dog's jaws, and its clingy texture can wreak havoc on your terrier's pearly whites. Use this type of food only as a last resort or as a supplement to your JRT's hard food.

WARNING

Feed your JRT on a regular schedule. Irregular feeding can affect her digestive system and can cause chronic digestive disorders. It also can make your dog frustrated and hungry.

Jack Russells are incredibly energetic. Studies have shown that their aerobic capacity exceeds that of humans by more than 200 percent, especially during exercise. Like humans, however, they need a proper balance of protein, carbohydrates, and fat. The meat in dog foods provides the protein your high-octane Jack Russell needs. Many of the best dog foods on the market advertise their high-protein content as a selling point — and with good reason. Protein is the foundation upon which your dog's growth and well-being is built. Dogs are *omnivores* (eating both plant and animal products), but they primarily are *carnivorous* (meat-eating) by nature. The protein derived from meat is more easily digested and is of higher quality than plant protein. Fat is also an important factor in your dog's diet, as are minerals and vitamins. Minerals and vitamins are easily overlooked, but they also should be part of the equation.

The selection of dog food on supermarket shelves is mind-boggling. There is "gourmet" food as well as food for dogs under stress, for puppies, for dogs that hunt, for fat dogs, for pregnant dogs, for skinny dogs, for middle-aged dogs, and for elderly dogs. The list is endless. Then there is the choice between dry food, semimoist food, and canned food. Naturally, each has pros and cons (see the "Dry, canned, or semimoist" sidebar for more information).

While scraps from the table are okay as an occasional treat, don't let them become a regular part of your dog's diet. Your intentions may be good, but you actually could be giving your terrier a case of gas or diarrhea as soon as the foreign food works its way through your JRT's system. But who can resist those begging eyes as you wolf down your pizza or the last bite of a hot dog without sharing with your pet? Give in when you must, but try to keep these kinds of treats to a minimum.

WARNING

Don't indulge your terrier by feeding her sweets. Contrary to popular belief, these treats don't cause worms, but they can cause tooth decay, stomach upset, and gas. And chocolate is poisonous to most dogs.

REMEMBER

The diet you feed your active, growing puppy during her first year is very important. Make sure she gets several smaller meals rather than one or two large ones.

Understanding Your Puppy's Feeding Needs

A puppy will multiply her birth body weight eight times before becoming a full-grown dog, so you want to feed your puppy a formula specifically designed for her growing needs to ensure a healthy, happy puppy and, eventually, a healthy, well-formed dog.

Puppies get all their nourishment from their mothers until they're about four weeks old. Around that time, the breeder begins to introduce puppy foods. After you bring your puppy home, it's up to you to select a dog food geared to your growing little bundle's nutritional needs. Although protein is very important in your puppy's growth and development, some evidence suggests that too much protein can cause skeletal, joint, and ligament problems. Your puppy's food should be balanced with vitamins, minerals, fats, carbohydrates, and proteins. When in doubt, choose a dog food that your veterinarian recommends and stick with it.

Puppies, like small children, have tiny stomachs. Feed your baby dog small quantities of puppy food several times a day instead of expecting her to get her nutritional needs from one big meal. It's a good idea to mix dry and canned meat food to create a blend that your puppy will enjoy. Be sure to remove the dish about 15 to 20 minutes after your dog has eaten, discard the unused food and serve fresh food at the next feeding. After the puppy is eating well, feed her dry food only but continue to feed her several times a day. This way, your puppy learns to eat when she's hungry without gorging herself whenever food is in sight. The puppy will gradually reduce her food intake to twice a day.

JRTs are active little dogs; rarely will you see an overweight JRT puppy unless she's being fed something other than dog food pellets. I don't recommend feeding your JRT scraps from your dinner, as you're eating. In no time, you'll create a begging puppy who is sure to grow into a full-fledged begging hound.

After one year, you can begin to introduce your puppy to adult dog food. Be sure to do so gradually, however, and make sure she has plenty of water to drink with her food. You also can feed your puppy in her crate. This helps create the feeling that the crate is a good place to be, and the dog gradually looks forward to meals in her own private dining room. As an added bonus, this acclimates your puppy to the crate for future fun trips with you.

If you have more than one puppy or dog, give each her own food and water bowls. This prevents fighting over food or one puppy getting more to eat than another. If one dog has a weight problem or is significantly bigger than the other, separate them when you feed them so that each dog eats only her share.

Making Adult Dinners

Just like humans, it isn't healthy for a dog to be overweight. Like you, your dog is what she eats. Don't fall for the myth that, if you want a strong, healthy dog, you must feed her plenty of meat and feed it often. Your terrier's appearance is a pretty good indication of her health. If you're starting to see dramatic weight gain or scratchy spots on her coat, the dog food you've chosen may be the culprit.

Feed your adult dog kibble or dry food as her basic meal, and remember to buy the best you can afford. In the long run, this food will save you money in vet bills. Another benefit of premium food is that your dog needs less food to feel full than with a cheaper brand. Premium dog foods have all the nutrients your dog needs, other than the water you provide. Barring specific problems, your adult dog won't need additional vitamin or mineral supplements. An acceptable premium dog food should contain 22 to 26 percent protein and 12 to 15 percent fat for both puppies and adults and should provide all of the vitamins and minerals that the dog needs. Look for a food that's easily digested and has been tested as having a low probability for food allergies.

Watching for weight loss . . .

Naturally, your Jack Russell's food requirements vary depending on her level of activity, her stress level, and her health. A lactating dam feeding seven puppies needs to eat more often than an adult male, and outdoor pets require more fuel than indoor dogs. Jack Russells who are active in show and hunting competitions require the most calories, and the quality of dog food becomes even more important for these active athletes. If your terrier is involved in any of these activities, watch her closely to make sure she doesn't drop weight.

Be aware that some terriers can lose weight rapidly. A dramatic weight loss is usually caused by an increase in exercise with no corresponding increase in food intake but can also be caused by illness. If you know that your dog will be changing her activity level, increase her food quality or amount just prior to undertaking the activity. If no such change has occurred, your terrier may have a digestive tract problem and should be taken to the vet for diagnosis. It's not normal for your JRT to experience significant weight fluctuations, and your dog should be evaluated by a professional if this occurs.

WARNING

Never feed your Jack Russell bones from chicken, pork, lamb, or fish because they can penetrate your dog's intestine or stomach and can be fatal. Also avoid chocolate, raw meat, and alcohol. Dogs have died as the result of their owner's misguided sense of humor in giving them alcohol.

. . . And for weight gain

If it looks like your dog is getting a bit pudgy and you can't afford a membership to the nearest canine gym, slowly decrease her food intake and increase her exercise. You can accomplish this by playing ball in your yard, taking trips to the nearest park, going on more frequent beach excursions, or taking additional walks — anything that provides some added physical exertion in your terrier's day. Remember, your JRT is high energy by nature. If you make the commitment to own a Jack Russell, you make the commitment to provide a suitable, healthy environment. If the pudginess continues, consult your veterinarian.

Because of their energy level, young and middle-aged Jack Russell Terriers rarely have a problem with obesity as long as they are on a healthy diet and have plenty of room to run and play. If your dog's coat seems lackluster and her energy level is low, don't take it upon yourself to add vitamins or minerals to her diet. Consult your vet for the appropriate course of action. These problems can be signs of something more serious.

REMEMBER

If a weight gain occurs due to fewer calories being burned, this places additional stress on your dog's heart and lungs.

Playing dinnertime hijinks

WARNING

Many Jack Russells are hit-and-run eaters. Their favorite method of dining is to go to the dog food bowl, take out four or five nuggets of food, walk to the nearest carpet, drop the nuggets and eat them one by one. They then walk back to the bowl and repeat the procedure. If your terrier is one of these sniper eaters, it doesn't matter how hungry she is or how hard you try to convince her otherwise — she won't stay at the bowl and chow down. This is why you're wise to place your terrier's food bowl on some type of carpet. Not all JRTs eat using this method, but it's prevalent enough to be worth mentioning.

Looking at Options for Older Dogs

Modern veterinary science has progressed by leaps and bounds to protect the health of older dogs and to increase their longevity. Now, more than ever, it's imperative that you shun cheaper dog food and stick to what your Jack Russell is used to. Keep in mind that, as you terrier gets older and less active, she should consume fewer calories to keep her from getting fat or even obese. Like all older dogs, even JRTs slow down a little as they mature. Keep an eye on your dog's weight to prevent any weight problem.

Older dogs often develop kidney problems, so feed your aging JRT lower levels of protein to guard against this. The protein doesn't cause kidney dysfunction, but high levels of protein can escalate an existing problem. Like a puppy, feed your older Jack Russell smaller meals more often. Keep dietary fat, especially human food scraps, to a minimum.

Don't forget to provide plenty of steady, low-impact exercise for your aging terrier. Just because she's slowing down a bit doesn't mean she wants to become a couch potato. Older terriers still love to go on walks and to play a toned-down game of fetch. They still can accompany you on trips to the park and will want to be included in your daily activities. Just use common sense to know when to quit and make sure your older JRT doesn't get overheated.

Internal body changes occur as your dog ages, resulting in decreased utilization and intestinal absorption of nutrients. If your JRT's digestive system becomes less efficient as your terrier gets older, your dog may have difficulty maintaining her body weight. This is when, under your veterinarian's supervision, you may want to give vitamin and mineral supplements.

WARNING

Don't punish your older JRT if she relieves herself in the house. Older Jack Russells can lose control of their bladders as they age, and they aren't soiling the house on purpose. They simply can't control their bladders long enough to head outside. Check with your vet to see if medications to control incontinence are appropriate for your dog.

Chapter **12**

Exercising Your Jack Russell

This book discusses how to train your JRT puppy, how to make your home a safe haven for your terrier, and some of the things to watch out for when working with your Jack Russell Terrier. But what are some of the ways to have loads of fun with both your terrier and your family and still keep everyone safe? The only limitation is your imagination.

Bouncing Balls

Talk to any Jack Russell Terrier owner and he will likely tell you that his JRT's favorite toy is a ball of some sort. The ball can be hard or soft, old or new, big or small; regardless of her size or texture, your Jack Russell Terrier will absolutely love it. Unlike your child's favorite toy that was outgrown within a few months, a JRT's ball is a toy for life. Terriers who are old and gray still respond to a ball with the same glee and excitement as a six-month-old puppy. Don't you wish your children were so easy to please?

The type of ball you choose depends on your needs and your plans for her use. If you plan to leave the ball on your living room floor or in your yard so that your dog has easy access to a play toy, choose a ball made of tough nylon. These balls are made with strong jaws in mind and can withstand the rigors of constant chewing. Keep in mind, though, that these tough balls always should be rolled and should never be thrown or used for catch. Because they are extremely hard, you can unintentionally injure your dog by accidentally hitting her, or your JRT can break a tooth by trying to catch the ball in midair.

TIP

Be sure the ball you choose for your dog is specifically made for dogs. Although standard tennis balls and racquetball balls are easy to buy and use, they're not usually made of material that's safe for ingestion by your dog. Stick to balls that are labeled as being safe for dogs.

Other balls, such as the balls made with softer nylon or polyurethane, are great for throwing. They bounce and are soft on your terrier's mouth for catching, but they can't take being constantly gnawed on. Plan to use these balls for games of fetch and toss (where you're in possession of the ball most of the time) and be sure to put the ball in a safe place that's out of reach from your terrier when you're through playing catch.

Balls made of other substances — such as string, cotton, and plastic — also work well for structured play, provided they're put away afterward. Don't forget that your crafty Jack Russell will remember where you hide her favorite ball, and any hiding place should be secure and safe enough that your terrier can't injure herself by trying to get to it.

TRY THIS

Use your imagination when playing ball with your Jack Russell Terrier. No one says it has to be a simple game of throw the ball and bring it back. Try playing ball inside your house, where the ball can ricochet down hallways or into different rooms. Your JRT will be amused for hours chasing and trying to find the ball when it seemingly disappears behind an open door. You also can bounce the ball on the ground, encouraging your JRT to jump up after it. Because Jack Russells are natural jumpers, they love to watch the ball bounce and try to gauge when the perfect time is to jump up and meet the ball on the way down. I guess you could say this increases eye-mouth coordination!

REMEMBER

Choose your ball-playing area with care and never throw the ball where it could pose a danger for your terrier. When a JRT plays ball, she's oblivious to anything else and can easily be hit by a car if you're not watching out for her safety.

When playing outside, the possibilities for fun are almost limitless. Throw the ball against a fence to really make your JRT jump, or teach her to wait away from you as you throw the ball high into the air for her to catch. Active JRTs love this game and will run at full speed. They carefully watch the air so they can time both their distance and their jump departure to perfectly match the course of the ball in the air.

For added fun, get several dogs involved (after proper introduction, of course) and have a race to see who can get to the thrown ball the quickest. You can arrange an obstacle course in which the dogs have to go through, over, or around one or more obstacles to fetch the ball. It's fun to see which dog figures this out first (though it's likely to be your own terrier). Enjoy your dog and enjoy being creative with her. This enjoyment will make your play time more fun and enjoyable for both you and your pooch.

Frisbee Fun

Like balls, your Jack Russell loves a good game of Frisbee. Whether in the park or in your backyard, JRTs have a natural propensity to watch things and, coupled with their extraordinary jumping ability, are naturals for catching flying, spinning objects. Using a Frisbee made just for dogs adds an even more amusing element because these Frisbees have *mouth-holds* that make the Frisbee easier to catch and hold than Frisbees made only for human hands. Your terrier is likely to add even more fun to the game by learning to toss and catch the Frisbee all by herself.

Although playing Frisbee inside may prove difficult without rearranging all the valuables in your living room, possibilities abound outside. You can use the Frisbee for long, bounding sprints or for sky-high catch targets. You even can roll it on edge on the ground; this makes for a great spinning, rolling toy. (You may already be well aware of how much JRTs like objects that look like wheels!) Regardless of how you use the Frisbee, encourage your terrier to leap, jump, run, and catch. You will have a healthy, happy terrier when she return to the confines of your home.

REMEMBER

Make sure your JRT is always wearing an ID tag that contains your address and phone number for quick identification should she become separated from you.

Running, Jet Setting, and Other Amusements

Although your Jack Russell Terrier is small, she's blessed with a huge heart in her chest, not to mention a huge lung capacity. Remember that these dogs were bred to go on the hunt and to run with the hounds in search of their prey. Not only do they have a virtually boundless energy supply, their potential for extreme physical fitness also is very strong.

If you're an outgoing family by nature — and hopefully you are if you've chosen to own a JRT — you should have no problem finding ways to exercise and enjoy your terrier. Likewise, your terrier should have no problem keeping up with your busy lifestyle and is likely to thrive in such a bustling, active environment.

REMEMBER

Don't feel as if you will wear out your terrier. This really isn't likely. Instead, take your canine friend with you as much as possible, and you will learn to love her company and the attention you get when your terrier steps out on the town with you. Because of their size, JRTs are easy to take along in a car, and they love to watch and smell anything and everything around them.

WARNING

Don't leave your Jack Russell in your car for any length of time on a warm day. An errand that takes "just a few minutes" can prove fatal to your pet.

Any outdoor jaunt can prove interesting for your terrier and fun for you, provided you have spent some time teaching your dog the basics of good doggy citizenship and pick up after her should nature call while you're out and about. Introduce your JRT to new people and dogs slowly to make sure the meeting goes well and keep your dog on a leash if she's outside your car and in an unenclosed area. You may be surprised at how many people recognize your feisty little terrier, even though they may not know the actual name of the breed.

REMEMBER

Whenever you take your terrier with you for a day of fun and exercise, bring along plenty of water and, if the day is hot, allow rest periods in the shade. Your JRT has lots of stamina, but she isn't Superdog and can end up with heat stroke if pushed too hard.

On the run

Running is a wonderful pastime for both you and your JRT. Unless you're a world-class runner, however, you will probably find that your terrier can outlast you even on your best days. Not only will your JRT keep up with you, you may find yourself pushing a little harder or a little farther to see if you actually can wear the little bugger out!

As an added bonus, other people will love your terrier's bouncy, energetic nature. Bringing your pooch along enables you to meet all sorts of new and fun people. And if somewhere down the line you do need protection, your canine bodyguard is just the length of a leash away. Don't be fooled by your JRT's happy nature. She can turn into a very effective and protective guard dog if she feels your safety is threatened.

Biking

Biking also can be a good, shared hobby if you take the time to teach your terrier the rules of the road and if you aren't going on a marathon ride. Be sure your dog is totally comfortable on a leash and is well schooled in the heel command. When this is accomplished, begin taking her out for short jaunts with your bike and keep your speed slow should your terrier mistakenly dart out in front of you. As your terrier begins to understand what's expected of her, she will stay next to you as you bike along. Keep in mind, however, that your terrier is running much farther than if you were running, so keep your distances within reason for your dog.

Swimming

Although running and biking may be just the right exercise for your terrier and your family, some folks are more adventurous than others. If you enjoy going for long days at the beach, water-skiing at the nearest lake, or fishing in a fabulous mountain river, will your JRT fit into this lifestyle? The answer is a resounding yes! The more the little whirlwinds are outside, the better they behave at home.

Oceanography 101

If you're lucky enough to live near the ocean and go there often, your terrier will be a lucky dog indeed. Although not in the same class as a retriever, terriers do well in water and are natural-born swimmers. They love to snap and bark at the white foam of the ocean waves and will be satisfied for hours by bouncing, playing, and romping through the water.

Children and JRTs (with adult supervision) love a day together at the beach. By allowing your terrier and your children to play together in the surf, you're strengthening the bond between your family members and are giving both your children and your terrier valuable exercise at the same time.

TIP

Frisbees are wonderful on the beach, and the sand provides secure footing with plenty of cushion for your high-flying terrier. Because the footing is deeper than in a park or in your backyard, your JRT gets the benefit of more cardiovascular exercise without the damage that hard-packed dirt or other abrasive surfaces can cause. Don't be afraid to use this to your advantage and to provide plenty of opportunities for your JRT to run and jump while visiting the beach.

TIP

Going to the beach takes a bit of planning. The last thing you want is for your fun day in the sun to turn into a sandy mess to clean up later or, worse, a dog or child with heat stroke and in need of medical attention. If you think ahead and plan the details of your trip in advance, however, you will reap a day of laughter, relaxation, and fun. (You may even catch your kids and terrier snoring away by the time you head home.) The following list can help, as can the "What to pack for the beach" sidebar.

>> Bring some zinc or strong sunscreen with you to the beach. Because your terrier is primarily white, the sun can wreak havoc on her delicate facial skin. If you notice the skin on your JRT's face starting to get pink, put some sunscreen on her.

>> Don't neglect your terrier's feet when on the beach. Remember that sand can heat up in a hurry and can cause sunburn and cracking of your terrier's pads. Keep your Jack Russell in wet sand whenever possible. If you find that your bare feet are being burned, either move to a shadier spot or take a break until things cool down.

>> Fleas can and do live in the sand in some areas. Flea-allergy dermatitis (FAD) can pop up on your pet after a day at the beach. If your terrier suddenly has itchy spots near her tail or at the base of her neck accompanied by hair loss, flea saliva could be the culprit (see Chapter 10).

Lakeside fun

As with beaches, lakes are great fun for terriers, especially because they're often nestled among the trees and brush — another favorite JRT play site. Because you don't have to worry about tides, you can safely play more fetching games in a lake than in the surf. Your dog can get a low-impact, high-cardiovascular workout all at once (see Figure 12-1)!

TIP

Bring small, floating balls and lures (such as empty water bottles) for your dog fetch or look around in the woods for several light sticks to throw. (The advantage of balls and lures is that they're usually brightly colored and are easier to find should they be misplaced or thrown out of sight.)

Before going to the beach, teach your JRT that, not only is it important to fetch the ball or stick, it is equally important to bring it back to you and to release it upon command. This game usually is easy to teach, especially in an enclosed yard with a long training lead. Your terrier can be fetching like a pro with very little time spent on training. Don't get angry with your dog for hanging onto a ball or a stick. To your dog, the stick now belongs to her, and she sees no good reason to give it up to you. When your terrier understands that if she drops the stick she'll have another chance to fetch it, she will be much more willing to give up its possession.

FIGURE 12-1:
Play fetch with
your JRT in any
nearby lake.

The river wild

If your family enjoys fishing, you may be glad to know that Jack Russell Terriers fit in quite nicely with this lifestyle. With knowledge of some basic commands (see Chapter 8), your JRT will undoubtedly be your willing companion on your fishing excursions, provided you won't get too angry should she begin barking and scare your fish away from time to time.

WARNING

Raging rivers move swiftly, and your curious terrier may inadvertently stumble into the current. Be careful when exposing your terrier to this type of water fun. A quiet, slow-moving river or stream, however, is enjoyable to your JRT.

Swimming pool stints

If you or a friend has a pool, your water fun could be as close as your own backyard. Terriers can enjoy the water here as easily as elsewhere (see Figure 12-2). Don't hesitate to introduce your terrier to your swimming pool for lots of summer family fun.

As with other bodies of water, make sure you introduce your terrier to your swimming pool gently. Show her where the steps are so that she can easily get in and out. Some dogs take to swimming pools very quickly; others are a bit intimidated and can take longer to get comfortable. Regardless of how long it takes, be patient!

WHAT TO PACK FOR THE BEACH

The first item to pack is your dog crate to transport your JRT to and from the beach and to use for a time-out, if needed. A create also comes in handy to cool off a JRT on the verge of heat stroke. Note that you'll have a far easier time ridding a dog crate of sand than your car upholstery and carpeting. Although some amount of sand debris should be expected after a trip to the beach, you may as well keep the cleanup to a minimum.

Use a terrycloth towel to line your Jack Russell's crate. Not only is it easy to clean, it also can double as a drying towel after your dog's day of water play. Fleece or other soft blankets work well at other times for your JRT's crate, but they trap sand particles like glue. Terry towels are easy to shake out and still provide plenty of cushioning for your JRT.

As with all traveling, bring plenty of food and water with you and don't rely on the water provided from the fountains or showers on the beach. Even if the beach is located in the same city, the water supply may be different and can upset your terrier's tummy on the way home. (Don't forget to bring a few bowls.)

Don't forget to put a sun umbrella in your beach suitcase. Not only does it provide shade for you and your children, your Jack Russell may need a shade break, as well. When taking your family to the beach, try to avoid the heat of the day and use the umbrella if the activity level gets hot and heavy. If you notice your terrier's tongue hanging well out of her mouth, and if she's breathing heavily after playing, it is a very good time for a break from the activity and a hefty drink of water.

FIGURE 12-2:
Try using a pool to help your JRT get exercise.

© Jackie and James Skaggs

Don't let your terrier have access to a swimming pool without supervision. Although she may be quite adept at swimming, she may inadvertently fall in and have a hard time getting back out. Be sure the gate to the pool is securely locked if your JRT is in the yard and you will be away from home. Also take the following precautions when playing in a pool with your JRT:

>> **Point out the exit:** Unlike lakes and beaches, swimming pools usually have only one easy way out for your dog. Even if your terrier is accustomed to swimming elsewhere, she may panic when she discovers that the sides of the pool are steep and that she can't get out wherever she chooses. This is why it is important for you to spend some time with your JRT, teaching her exactly where the steps are and that there's no need to panic.

If the pool's steps are of the ladder type instead of being built in, a makeshift wooden ramp will enable your dog to easily get in and out of the pool. As long as your dog understands that she's not trapped in the water, it usually will relax and enjoy swimming with you and your family.

>> **No Marco Polo:** If children will be playing in the pool with your dog, teach both the children and the dog that you have swimming pool rules. Don't allow your children to throw your terrier into the pool. Even the best of swimmers can be startled by suddenly flying through the air and landing abruptly in the water.

Be sure your children understand that your dog has sharp claws. In the course of swimming or trying to get out, the dog may unintentionally scratch their young, sensitive skin. Make a rule that, if the dog is in the pool, the children shouldn't interfere with her swimming by trying to hold or carry her in the water.

Some Jack Russells love to dive after rocks and balls. Make sure your children know to let your dog surface if she's going after a rock, and that she only can hold her breath for so long. If they don't understand this, your dog may drown while your children are trying to play with her.

Remember that pools contain chemicals. Too much exposure to these chemicals can cause eye and skin irritations in your Jack Russell. Keep pool swim time to no more than an hour and keep an eye on your terrier's coat and eyes to make sure they aren't unduly sensitive. If you notice a rash on her skin or tearing of the eyes, discontinue your JRT's swimming privileges for a while to see if these symptoms clear up. If they don't, you may have to limit or discontinue your dog's pool activities. Always check your pool's chemical level before use to make sure the chlorine and pH factors are in the normal range. Don't allow your terrier to swim if you've recently added chemicals.

SWIMMING GUIDELINES

Don't throw your dog into the water unless you know for a fact that she's comfortable with swimming and can find her way out. Although terriers have a natural propensity and understanding of the basics of swimming, many have never been exposed to large bodies of water and may panic when they're suddenly thrown in and told to sink or swim.

A dog who is panicking will not enjoy swimming. This type of introduction to water can lead to a Jack Russell who won't go anywhere near the water despite its natural proclivity to do so. Be sensitive to your dog and introduce her to water slowly. Better yet, throw a ball or lure and let your JRT decide for herself when is the right time to go in after it.

Horsing around

JRTs and horses seem to go together like birds of a feather (see Figure 12-3). A JRT can be a wonderful help around the barn, keeping the area free of the rats and mice that love to chew holes in feed sacks and leather tack. Most horses accept the presence of these terriers with remarkable ease. Even grumpy horses that don't particularly care for dogs are tolerant of these zippy white streaks that go running through their stalls. Even when they chase the dogs out of their pens, it's with only half-hearted threats. If you do decide to take your JRT out to visit a ranch, make sure dogs are allowed on the property and watch your dog closely to be sure she doesn't get herself into trouble.

The number of Jack Russell Terriers purchased by horse owners across the United States has grown dramatically in the past several years. Many horse owners are accustomed to having these little dogs around and welcome their company, provided they behave themselves and aren't unruly or destructive. My JRTs accompany me on trail rides with several of my horses, keeping up easily with my mounts and always uncannily knowing where the horses' feet will land.

The biggest danger you face with your terrier and horses is the unintentional kick by a horse and the damage it can cause. Horses have several visual blind spots and sometimes are taken unaware by a dashing white terrier. Kicks usually occur around feeding time or when the horse is in a large area at play, so take special care at these times to protect your dog. Don't allow your JRT to enter an arena or pasture area and keep her safely outside the fence. If your terrier doesn't quickly learn to stay outside of these boundaries, keep her on a leash when horses are out running around or trying to eat. This will help protect your dog from harm and you from an unnecessary vet bill.

FIGURE 12-3:
Horses and Jack
Russells are
natural pairs.

© Ken and Donna Dannen/AKC Stock Images

WARNING

If your dog suddenly starts limping, check all four legs and paws for obvious causes such as a torn toenail or a foxtail between her toes. If you can find nothing of this sort and the lameness doesn't resolve itself within a day, call your vet and schedule an appointment. Your dog may have torn a ligament or received a kick from a horse that you're unaware of.

Dog Parks

A trip to the park can be a great outlet for both your family and your dog. Because parks offer lots of the wide-open space usually unavailable in a backyard, they provide your terrier with a super opportunity to run and play. Parks are great for playing ball and Frisbee or even for a good game of chase. Your children and your terrier will enjoy just being out and about in the fresh air and sunshine.

Many suburban neighborhoods are now building enclosed areas within their local parks specifically for doggy exercise. These safe, fenced runs are quite large, and they allow for either solitary play or introduction to other dogs using the facility, depending on the wishes of the individual dog owners. Because the areas are safely fenced, you can let your dog run and be secure in the knowledge that it can't get into trouble, and you can focus your energy on getting the most play and exercise for your dog.

TAKING YOUR TERRIER ALONG

Whatever your favorite outdoor activity, try to include your JRT. Not only will you enjoy her company on the trip, your terrier will enjoy spending time with you and exercising at the same time. This will lead to a stronger bond between your dog, and your family will give you lots of fond memories of your trips. It has the added bonus of relieving much of your dog's pent-up energy, and it's likely to provide a happier, more relaxed terrier at home, as well.

WARNING

Don't lose track of your dog while she's playing, however. Cleaning up after her is still your responsibility, even at a doggy park.

REMEMBER

Don't assume that every dog owner in the park is interested in helping you socialize your terrier. If you see two dogs who appear to get along and are playing well together, ask the owner or owners whether they mind if your dog joins in. Keep your JRT on a leash through the introductions and be willing to back away should things look less than promising. (Note, however, that dogs are far more likely to be aggressive to other dogs when on leash than when off. If you and the other dog owner are willing, you may want to try an introduction without a leash on either dog.)

These parks are a wonderful way to socialize your potentially antisocial Jack Russell because you can introduce her to one or two new dogs at a time. You're also in a confined area where you can easily reach your dog and can pull her out of trouble if necessary. Not only that, parks take some of the exercise burden off your shoulders by allowing your dog to romp and run with other dogs, minimizing your constant involvement. By staying close by, your JRT can check on you periodically yet can still enjoy the company and roughhousing of other energetic doggy playmates.

Nature at Its Best

If hiking and camping are your speed, you'll find that your Jack Russell Terrier is just as at home in the great outdoors as she is on the beach or in the park. Terriers love to hunt and explore; being able to do so while accompanying you on a walk only adds to her pleasure. Be careful, though, that you've done all your basic obedience work at home and have thoroughly schooled your terrier in both the heel and come commands.

Because JRTs are natural hunters, the call of the wild will be stronger while in the great outdoors than at home or in a park. Your terrier can easily get herself into trouble by running off after a squirrel or by poking her head down the wrong hole.

The safest bet is to explore an area with your terrier safely in tow before letting her off the leash. Be sure there are no busy roads around the next bend or a swift running river at the bottom of the hill. Only let her off leash when you're confident that she'll be under control.

Keep in mind that a terrier's hunting instincts are very strong. The main thing on her mind will be to find a squirrel or another enticing rodent to chase. This could lead your dog right into the clutches of a poisonous snake or some other hidden peril, and she may not respond quickly enough to your calls if she's in the heat of a hunt. You dog also could stumble over an embankment or fall into an unseen hole while running after some small animal. If this were to happen, it would be hard to find your dog without some serious searching and a whole lot of luck.

Avoid any thickly wooded areas or spaces with abundant small game unless you have your terrier on a leash. This will prevent her from running off after a rustling in the brush that is sure to lead to another rustling in the brush. Eventually, your dog will be far away from camp with no idea how she got there or how to find her way back. By the time your JRT wakes up and realizes she has traveled too far afield, she may be out of shouting distance. Finding your Jack Russell could be like finding the proverbial needle in a haystack.

REMEMBER

Check your dog for nicks and ticks after a walk in the woods. Ticks can harbor diseases and can cause irritations in your dog's skin (see Chapter 10), and nicks should be treated promptly.

Winter Wonderland

Jack Russells are more water and warm-weather dogs than they are snow bunnies, but they can enjoy the sticky white stuff, as well. Take a few extra precautions to ensure your dog's comfort and use common sense about how long to expose your terrier to the elements.

The Jack Russell Terrier's coat was meant to protect the dog from the elements; therefore, the coat has some natural water-wicking properties. Although England is hardly in a warm climate, terriers were found by the hearth during inclement weather more often than they were found hunting foxes in the snow. Because a JRT's coat is thinner than her snow-loving canine counterparts, your JRT should be equipped with a warm sweater or a doggy coat to help keep her body heat up when out in snow or very cold weather. If you plan to play in the snow for a long period of time (such as an hour or two), provide some type of protection for your terrier's paws to prevent freezing and cracking caused by ice crystals.

REMEMBER

Remember that your terrier isn't a Husky or St. Bernard. If you intend to take her into the snow or ice, provide plenty of protection to keep her warm and keep her moving to elevate her body temperature.

If your terrier starts shaking, even with a sweater or coat on (see Figure 12-4), she's probably too cold. If you've been standing still for a period of time, increase your terrier's activity level to get her muscles moving and her heart pumping. This will raise her core temperature and may be enough to keep her warm. If your terrier keeps shivering in spite of these efforts, do the humane thing and bring her in out of the cold.

FIGURE 12-4:
A sweater keeps your JRT a bit warmer on chilly days.

© Mark Hay

What can you do in the winter months when neither of you is interested in braving the elements to fit in a little exercise? Are you doomed to months of dealing with a hyperactive terrier? Or are there toys made specifically for indoor play? Of course there are, and some may be as close as your nearest toy store.

Laser tag

Jack Russells are fascinating little creatures, and they are amused by a wide variety of play toys. From motorized stuffed animals to tiny laser beams of light, indoor playtime can be just as satisfying and as exhausting as an outdoor romp for your terrier. It just takes a little ingenuity on your part and a ready-to-play terrier.

WOODSY WARNINGS

WARNING

Be sure to check your dog several times each day for ticks that can attach to her skin while banging through the brush. Some ticks, especially deer ticks, carry serious diseases that may affect your terrier's health should she be bitten. Even if the tick doesn't carry a disease, your JRT can have a nasty reaction and start swelling if the tick isn't removed promptly.

Don't forget to check inside your dog's ears and under her tail when looking for these nasty little creatures. These are easy places to miss and are ones where ticks love to hide. Pull the tick out slowly with a pair of tweezers and kill it between two rocks or with the sole of your shoe. If you notice severe swelling, a fever, or listlessness in your dog shortly after a tick bite, call your veterinarian for further advice or treatment.

Other dangers when camping or hiking include cuts and tears to your dog's feet and legs that are caused by rocks and sharp brush. As with ticks, be sure to check your dog's feet and legs several times a day or if you notice your dog limping. Many times the culprit is a splinter, a foxtail between your terrier's toes, or a nick on the foot or leg caused by a sharp rock or stick. If you find a foreign body lodged between the toes, remove it carefully and apply some antibiotic ointment. If you find a small cut, apply ointment and keep an eye on it. If your dog is limping badly or if the cut is accompanied by a significant amount of bleeding, stabilize the limb and contact a vet right away.

Because terriers love to dig in rabbit and squirrel holes and their excavation efforts are rarely subtle, they often end up with dirt and debris in their eyes. Your dog usually will be no worse for wear in these instances, but occasionally a particularly stubborn particle will work itself into an eye and cause the eye to tear or swell.

If you notice wetness around one of your terrier's eyes, explore further to see if she has something lodged between the eye and the lid. Don't use your finger or a sharp object to remove a particle. Instead, use saline solution to thoroughly rinse out your dog's eye and then check to see whether the particle has been removed. This prevents any scratching of the lens and aids the tearing that may occur when removing the foreign object from the eye.

One of the best toys on the market for your JRT's indoor amusement is the *pet laser.* This tiny toy leads to hours of fun and hilarity in your household, and your JRT will never tire of chasing it around the floor and up the walls. The toy is actually a small, cylindrical tube that holds a tiny light source. When turned on, a pin-point colored beam of light glows on whatever surface the light is aimed at. To your JRT, it looks like a bug on the wall or the floor. Given that most terriers are fascinated with hunting bugs or other such prey, this toy has become a favorite of Jack Russell Terrier owners across the nation.

You can use the pet laser to draw intricate patterns on the ground, up the walls, and even onto the ceiling, and your terrier terror will follow it every step of the way. Some JRTs get so intent on catching the elusive little light that they actually jump several feet off the ground trying to grab it from the wall or the ceiling. They go crazy until the light ends up back on the ground where they think they can reach it. All this usually keeps family members in hysterics as they watch the dog perform amazing acts of contortion in an effort to catch the tiny light beam. It's also highly amusing to friends and neighbors who have never seen this side of your JRT.

Other toys originally meant for human use, such as light sabers, cones, plastic wands, and the like, can keep your dog more than satisfied when the weather won't cooperate. Just go to the toy store with your dog in mind and make sure whatever you choose is durable enough to stand up to your dog's strong jaws. Remember never to leave such toys sitting about for your dog to chew on. They weren't made for this type of abuse, and your dog could be injured if she ingests part or all of such a toy.

Toys for tugging

Tug toys, cotton and plastic toys that are designed to give your terrier something to hold on to when you (or another dog) pulls on the other end, are great for your terrier. Be careful not to pull back too hard, however, because you may loosen your JRT's tooth. As long as your terrier is in control of the tension, however, you shouldn't have a problem. You'll probably be amazed at just how strong your Jack Russell really is.

TRY THIS

Two dogs together really can get a work out with tug toys. Put one dog on each end and watch the fun begin. They growl ferociously and pull back and forth, alternating with vicious shaking of their heads as if to kill the beast in their clutches. This is great fun for your terrier and is good for teeth cleaning, as well. The cotton acts as a dental cleaner, and the pulling action gives your dog's jaws a healthy round of exercise. Couple this with some rounds of fetch with the toy, and you can wear your JRT out in no time or at least get her a little tired. When the tug toy gets worn and ratty around the edges, throw it away and spring for a new one.

Chapter **13**

Grooming Your Jack Terrier

B ecause Jack Russells have reasonably short coats, caring for your terrier's coif, especially for a dog with a smooth coat, is fairly simple. But there is more to routine JRT health than an occasional bath, a good brushing, and a daily walk. Preventive maintenance and upkeep can prevent many health problems that, if left unchecked, can pose a problem for your JRT. It's a bit like taking your car to the garage for a lube job to prevent engine problems. Like your car, a well-tuned and well-cared-for Jack Russell will be a happy pet who will give you many years of love and devoted companionship.

Bathing Beauties

Depending on your Jack Russell's outside activities, you should only have to bathe him every month or less. Of course, if your terrier is out rolling in the dirt on a daily basis, you may have to bathe him a bit more frequently. Short, more frequent baths are better than long, infrequent ones. Get your dog used to baths when he's still a puppy. As with children, try to make bath time fun by combining it with a bit of playtime.

Don't banish your Jack Russell to the great outdoors when he smells a bit gamey. If a bath doesn't solve the problem and your terrier has had his regular dental cleanup, something else is wrong. A smelly dog is often a symptom of a more serious medical problem.

Preparing for the bath

Keep a large towel nearby to prevent having a wet and exuberant JRT running through the house spraying water everywhere. Don't be surprised if your terrier is overcome by a bout of Jack Russell "turboitis" immediately after his bath. Just smile as he rockets through the house and know that this is the reason you adopted a JRT in the first place.

Finding a shampoo and using it

Like all dog products on the market, you may find the selection of shampoos to be intimidating, but rest assured that most are fairly equal in effectiveness. A more costly shampoo isn't necessarily better than an inexpensive one.

TIP

One particularly useful item you may want to check out is a dry shampoo that requires no water or rinsing. If you and your terrier are always on the go, you may want to invest in this handy cleaning solution. You'll be glad you have it on hand when you have a filthy Jack Russell and bathing your dog with regular shampoo and water isn't feasible.

When using a shampoo with water, use one suited to your Jack Russell's coat or skin problems, if he has any. In other words, choose a moisturizing shampoo if his skin is dry and scaly or an oatmeal shampoo if your dog has a tendency to itch. Before beginnign the bath, check to see whether the water is warm but not hot. As you apply shampoo to his coat, work your way across his body, paying particular attention to the oily areas of his ears but avoiding the eyes. When rinsing, reverse the motion and rinse from head to rump, making sure that no shampoo residue remains.

Coat Care

All dogs shed, and your smooth-coated Jack Russell is no exception, so don't expect him to be "shed free." A good outside brushing with a bristle brush (see Figure 13-1) or a special mitt keeps your floors and carpets as free of hair as possible. It is perfectly okay to trim errant hairs on your dog's feet, rump, and abdomen area.

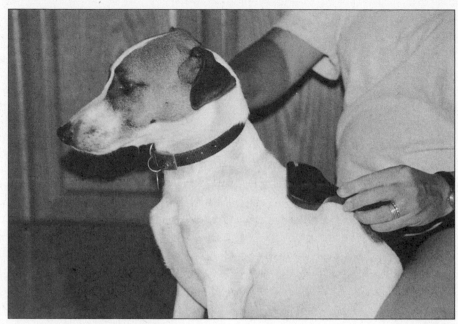

FIGURE 13-1:
Use a brush to keep your Jack Russell's coat smooth.

REMEMBER

Naturally, a rough or broken-coated Jack Russell requires a bit more care than one with a smooth coat. If you have a rough or broken-coated terrier, a stripping comb is a great help in plucking your dog's dead hair. If you're really big on coat care, you also may enjoy the convenience of a combing table if you have the room and can afford one. Just remember that grooming need not be a time-consuming experience. A thorough once-a-week brushing and a good vacuum job on the house should do just fine.

Tough Teeth

Dogs, like humans, have two sets of teeth. Their baby teeth, all 28 of them, come in when the puppy is between three and six weeks old and are replaced by 42 permanent teeth when your dog is about four months old. (Puppies can have a condition called *retained baby teeth*, in which they never drop their toddler teeth to make room for their adult counterparts. This condition can cause a bad bite, also called *malocclusion*, and misaligned adult teeth later on.) Your dog uses his incisors to nibble meat from bones and to groom himself, the canine teeth for holding things in his mouth and for defending himself as needed, and the premolars to rip meat off bones.

Just like humans, dogs are subject to tooth problems and require regular checkups and treatment. Don't allow dental care to slide — neglected plaque and tartar can cause infections along your dog's gumline. Your Jack Russell also can develop tooth decay.

Ideally, you should brush your dog's teeth daily (see Figure 13-2) using a child's toothbrush or one angled specifically for a dog's mouth and a toothpaste developed especially for dogs. If you don't have the time for such extensive dental care — and unfortunately most people don't — at least brush his teeth once a week and make sure your terrier has plenty of hard biscuits, rawhide, and other chewies to help remove plaque. If, despite your best efforts, plaque still accumulates, take your Jack Russell to the vet yearly to have the plaque removed. As your dog ages, you may want to have his teeth cleaned more often.

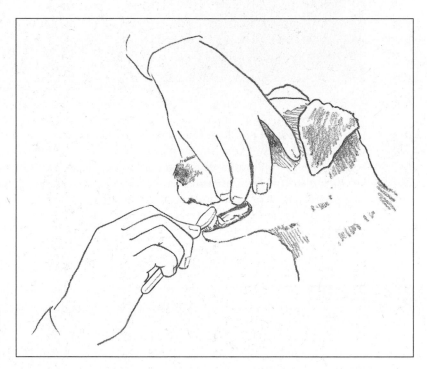

FIGURE 13-2:
Brush your Jack Russell's teeth regularly.

Dogs don't usually develop cavities, but if your dog eats too much soft food, debris can accumulate in pockets at the base of his teeth. This can cause infections that soften gums and cause them to recede. Ultimately, tooth loss may occur. In areas of hard water, tartar (the result of calcium salts' accumulation) also can be a problem. If severe, it may have to be removed by your vet. Mouth odor, a yellow-brownish crust of tartar around the gumline, and pain or bleeding of the gums are all signs of trouble. If noticed, attend to these symptoms immediately. Removing the plaque and treating other gum and dental problems usually requires that your dog be sedated. Have your vet explain any ill effects that can be expected from these procedures.

REMEMBER

Don't forget to care for your dog's teeth. Neglect can cause more than bad breath. It can result in a bacterial infection that can travel to your terrier's bloodstream and damage his heart's valves.

The Ears Have It!

To avoid an unexpected ear infection or an infestation of ear mites, check your Jack Russell's ears frequently. Because JRTs frequently are out running around, they're prone to picking up infections caused by dirt and debris getting trapped in their ear canals after vigorous bouts of digging. They also can pick up ear mites, which can make your terrier miserable if left untreated. Check your JRT's ears on a weekly basis. If you suspect that something is amiss, your vet can provide you with special ear drops to keep your dog's ears clean and wax free. Place a few drops in each ear, massage gently, and let the drops thoroughly penetrate.

REMEMBER

Parasites in your dog's ears can be a source of infection. You often can remove ticks that have made their way into your dog's ears yourself, but ear mites and other types of mites usually are more insidious and require professional treatment.

If you notice your dog pawing or scratching at his ears or shaking his head, it may be a sign of an ear infection. Redness and a smelly discharge also are signs that something isn't right and that your dog needs immediate attention. These symptoms often can be caused by foreign bodies or dirt in your dog's ear, a severe case of wax buildup, ear mites, a yeast infection, or *otitis*, which is an inflammation of the area outside the eardrum. Its symptoms are the same as those just described, and pus may be present in severe cases. In the case of ear mites, remember that they are very small and often are difficult to detect with the naked eye. In any case, contact your vet to diagnose the exact cause of the problem.

If you suspect your dog has a foreign object lodged in his ear, place a few drops of baby oil or mineral oil in the ear. Massage gently to soften the object and to relieve the pain until you can have the problem addressed by a trained professional. If you hike in rugged terrain where your dog may be apt to get twigs, dirt, or other foreign substances in his ears, wads of cotton are useful as a preventive measure. (Whatever you do, though, don't stick anything down deep into your dog's ear. You may push any wax or debris farther into the ear canal, making it more difficult to get out.)

The Pedicure

Nail clipping (see Figure 13-3) doesn't have to be traumatic for either of you, but you should exercise a bit of caution when trimming your JRT's nails yourself. If you begin clipping your dog's nails when he's a puppy, he will become accustomed to the process and will be less likely to object. Nonetheless, don't expect your Jack Russell to be overjoyed when he sees you approaching with clippers in hand. A treat will go a long way toward softening your dog's disposition and making him a bit more accepting of a pedicure.

To trim your terrier's nails, leave him on the ground to make him feel more secure. You also have a bit of an easier time if someone can keep your terrier distracted by feeding him treats and by keeping him from moving around. Start with the rear feet, grasping his foot gently but firmly with pads facing down. Work your way forward until all 16 toenails are clipped and accounted for. Talk to your dog in a low voice to reassure him that he has nothing to worry about. Give him a good hug and a treat when you're done to ease his traumatized mind.

TIP

If your Jack Russell is highly resistant to nail trimming, clip one or two nails per day, giving lots of treats. This makes nail trimming a more positive, less traumatic experience.

FIGURE 13-3:
Trim your JRT's toenails carefully.

The single-blade, guillotine-type nail clipper works best, but some people prefer the type that looks like diminutive pliers with a blade at top and bottom. Make sure the blades on the clippers are sharp. They'll cut faster, require less effort, and be less apt to pinch or smash the dog's nail, which can be very painful.

Don't clip the nail too close to the quick. A dog's nails contain nerves and blood. Cutting them too short will hurt your terrier, cause bleeding, and make your pet more resistant to the procedure in the future. You can easily distinguish the live part of the nail from the *dead part* (the part you want to cut) by holding your JRT's foot with the pad facing downward and observing which part of the nail is pink and which part is clear or white. The sensitive part (live part) is the red or pink part closest to the toe; the dead part is lower, toward the tip. For dogs with black toenails, trim carefully to avoid accidentally nipping too close to the live part.

When you're done, fuss over your dog and offer a treat. Soon your pet will become less resistant to nail cutting, making the entire experience more enjoyable for you both.

Chapter **14**

Competing in Trials

There are an endless number of ways in which you and your family can enjoy your dog. From playing and swimming in the backyard to beach and mountain excursions, your Jack Russell Terrier is happiest when he's at your heels. But what if you want to meet some other JRT owners to see just how your little white flash stands up to other feisty Jack Russells? The answer is just a trial away.

What's a Terrier Trial?

Jack Russell Terrier trials are organized activities designed specifically for JRT owners and their dogs. Some are sanctioned by the Jack Russell Terrier Club of America (JRTCA), some by the American Kennel Club (AKC), and still others are more like play days and anyone is welcome. The only requirement is that participants have or love Jack Russells. All JRT trials have one thing in common: They offer a variety of classes for Jack Russell owners to strut their stuff and to see just where their terriers' talents lie.

Included in most Jack Russell Terrier trials are *conformation* (judged on the dog's structure, breed characteristics, and movement), obedience, hunting (go to ground), racing, and agility competitions. The age, sex, height, and ability of the dogs can come into play in a particular type of competition. Regardless of which activity you choose, you're sure to find a classification in which your dog can naturally excel. The following sections look at each activity individually — you can decide which is the most interesting to you.

Conformation critique

When most people think of dog shows, they think of conformation or "breeding" classes. These beauty-pageant-like classes showcase the terrier who most closely matches the "ideal" for that particular registry or governing body. Much primping and preening goes on before a conformation competition, although perhaps less with JRTs than with other breeds of dogs. Spayed and neutered terriers aren't eligible in sanctioned competitions, although they are welcome in play-day classes (the only exceptions are Junior Handler, Veteran, and JRTCA Bronze Medallion classes).

The conformation classes are presided over by a judge and a ring steward, much like any other breed conformation class. Occasionally, these two officials are accompanied by an apprentice judge who is working to become a licensed judge. These individuals are responsible for making sure that the terriers are presented in an orderly fashion, that all rules are followed, and that the classes proceed in a timely fashion. The announcer provides an update on the classes about to come in and the results of the class in the ring.

Although the judge's view always is subjective, the purpose of the conformation class is to choose the dog who best represents the ideal Jack Russell Terrier, both in physical attributes and in temperament. Physical perfection certainly is the goal, but the terrier also must portray the essence of the working JRT to be considered ideal.

TIP

If you plan to show your terrier in conformation classes, make sure to get him used to standing quietly, working comfortably on a leash, and being approached and touched by strangers. It would be embarrassing (to say the least) if your dog bit the judge when she came over to inspect him!

REMEMBER

Judging the JRT is a hands-on experience. The judges not only want to view the terrier standing, walking, and trotting, they also *span* the terrier (check that the circumference of the dog's rib cage can easily be encircled by normal-sized hands). They do this by placing their hands around the terrier just behind the *withers* (the highest points of the shoulder blades), with their thumbs and little fingers touching. If they can accomplish this, the terrier is said to fit into the breed standard.

To make the class size equitable and manageable, classes traditionally are broken into divisions, including the following:

>> Puppy

>> Open adult

- >> Junior handler
- >> Working
- >> Miscellaneous

Cross entries aren't allowed within the open division. These classes often are further divided by height, coat type, and experience. Working dogs are required to satisfy hunting requirements before becoming eligible to be shown in that division. In JRTCA competitions, a Bronze Medallion class is often offered for terriers who have earned a JRTCA Bronze Medallion for special accomplishments in field work. Only dogs who satisfy the requirements can enter, and spayed and neutered dogs are allowed.

Only obedience

Obedience trials are a great way to show off how well you've trained your terrier. These classes require the terrier to perform several tests of obedience, and the dog and handler with the most points at the end of the class are declared the winners. The tests required depend on the sanctioning body under which you're competing.

PREPARING TO SHOW YOUR JRT

Although preparing your terrier for competing in conformation classes isn't quite as training intensive as some of the other trial divisions, you still must do some preparation before attempting to compete at a trial. Practice getting your terrier to walk briskly and dependably on a leash, to stand quietly on a table (though they sometimes are shown on the ground), and to allow himself to be checked and handled (including his teeth, ears, and tail). You should also make sure your terrier will act in an acceptable social manner when in the presence of other terriers.

Remember that your JRT should be in good physical shape when competing in conformation classes. This enhances his physical appearance and makes spanning him much easier. You want to present your dog in the best light possible, so don't scold or reprimand your terrier. Scolding will make your dog tuck or drop his tail, giving the appearance of a timid or unhappy dog. Keep ample space between yourself and the next dog and always be a good sport regardless of the judging results. Most of all, remember that you're doing this for fun. Winning a ribbon is never a life-or-death matter.

Classes are divided by skill level, and you may find separate divisions for juniors and adults. All dogs are required to perform a sequence of tests based on their training levels. A score is given for each element or test that reflects not only how well the dog performs the exercise but also his attitude in doing so. Unlike conformation classes, physical appearance is not a factor in judging this division. It only matters whether the terrier correctly completes the test and whether he displays a willing attitude toward the handler. Class size usually is limited so that the dogs focus more on their handlers than on the hubbub surrounding them and so that the classroom area isn't too crowded.

In novice or beginner classes, terriers are asked to perform heel, heel in a pattern (usually a figure eight), stand for examination, and come. All these commands are performed on a leash at least six feet long. Usually, the dogs also are asked to sit and stay and to down and stay for a specified period of time. They also may be asked to heel off the leash and to come off the leash depending on the class requirements and the preferences of the judge. All these skills are fundamentals that can be accomplished with some practice and diligence at home.

As the divisions increase, so does the skill level required. At higher levels, handlers may be asked to show that their dogs can heel while not on a leash, can perform a figure eight, can release a toy or dumbbell when asked, can retrieve an object and retrieve while performing jumps and long sits and downs.

TRY THIS

As the dogs move into the utility division, they're asked to display their understanding of hand signals, scent discrimination, and jumping and retrieving skills. These skills require substantial training and considerable expertise. If you're interested in competing at these levels, look for books and instructors that are specifically geared toward advanced obedience training to help you prepare for these competitions.

TIP

Be patient while training your JRT. Although these dogs are incredibly smart, it often is difficult for them to focus. Effective training makes use of a dog's favorite reward — be it a food treat, a toy, or praise.

Get down and go to ground!

The go-to-ground competition is unique to hunting dogs and can be an exciting competition to watch and participate in. It also can be extremely loud, so bring either earplugs or a big dose of tolerance for this event. Those very voices that make the dogs easy to find underground can be skull-splitting when used in chorus in anticipation of the hunt.

GETTING INVOLVED

You can contact several of your local clubs to find out when the next trials will be held and where the closest ones are to your home. Chapter 18 and the Appendix list a number of resources available to help you track down this information. Even if you're not sure that you're interested, go to one and see what it's all about. You may find that it is just the challenge you've been looking for!

The Jack Russell Terrier was bred to be the perfect subterranean hunting partner, and this competition puts these qualities to the test. The dog who will be most successful in this event is compact with balanced proportions, strong limbs, and a small chest that enables him to enter the squirrel or foxhole. Wherever the fox can go, the JRT must be able to follow. The terrier must be flexible enough to maneuver the twists and turns of the tunnels leading to the quarry's den and must be willing and able to bark loudly until found.

The go-to-ground trial event was developed to test these skills. Its sole purpose is to test the specific skills necessary for a JRT to successfully go down into the tunnel, scent out his prey, choose the correct paths to find the quarry, and work the quarry as would be needed during a real hunt. All go-to-ground courses are designed with these skills in mind.

As with other skill competitions, go-to-ground trials are divided into classes based on the age, size, and skill of the terriers competing, and the courses are designed with these class specifications in mind. The most common divisions are novice, puppy, open, advanced, championships, and size-split classes.

The courses consist of underground tunnels that have been designed specifically for this use. The more difficult the division, the more turns and dead-ends the terrier will have to navigate to reach his prey. The tunnels also get longer as the dogs move up into higher levels of competition. The quarry can be a squirrel, a rat, or another rodent suitable for the task. All of these animals are caged to prevent injury during the competition.

The go-to-ground competition has a set course of events that the promoters of the trial must follow. The terrier is placed at the opening of the tunnel with all four feet on the ground. The starter tells the handler to release the dog, and a stopwatch is started. It is the JRT's job to navigate the twists and turns of the tunnel and to locate the quarry as fast as he can. After he reaches the rodent, the terrier must bark, whine, scratch, or otherwise "mark" the quarry for a specific amount of time. After this is accomplished, the time is recorded and the next JRT is set loose on the course.

The JRT with the best time wins. If the terrier fails to find the quarry, doesn't mark it after he has found it, or leaves the tunnel more than once, the dog is disqualified (except in novice classes). The judge for the event is stationed at the finish line and makes sure the terrier works the prey for the allotted time before deeming the time as official. The ruling of the course judge is final.

This is a fun competition that requires very little preparation on your part, and it allows you to view your terrier in an environment that shows his remarkable natural hunting ability. It will certainly give you a newfound respect for your JRT's hunting skills and, perhaps, a new understanding of why barking and digging are so much a part of your Jack Russell's makeup. The only drawback is listening to all those terriers barking in anticipation of getting onto course!

REMEMBER

Schooling on the day of a go-to-ground trial isn't permitted.

Russell Racing

Perhaps one of the most fun and exciting events at the JRT trial is the racing competition. As a new Jack Russell Terrier owner, you may be surprised at how fast your dog can run while fetching a ball or chasing a cat. If you really want to see your dog in action, put your terrier into one of the racing competitions. You will be amazed at just how fast several JRTs racing against one another can go. They truly are just flashes of white when they really get going!

REMEMBER

Like the go-to-ground event (see the "Get down and go to ground!" section, earlier in this chapter), racing events can get very loud as the dogs bark in anticipation of running their race. Be prepared for this, lest you lose your patience and turn your fun day at the trial into a short-tempered shouting match.

Two types of races usually are offered at the trials: flat races and races over hurdles (steeplechase). As with the other competitions, races are divided in the standard ways by height, age, skill, and sex. Because speed is a factor and taller dogs have much longer legs than shorter dogs, all divisions usually are split by height as well to ensure an equitable race.

REMEMBER

If you decide to race your terrier, be prepared to cool him down at the end of the race either by dunking him or by pouring cold water over him. Sprinting is hard work and, coupled with the excitement of the other dogs, your terrier can easily get overheated.

Racing particulars

The course is 150 to 225 feet long and has a starting box at one end and a finish line at the other. The finish line usually is made from several bales of straw or hay with a hole in the middle. This provides a soft wall in the event that several careening JRTs make it to the end at the same time. A piece of fur or a squirrel's tail is used as a lure to get things going, and it is attached to a piece of rope or a string to be pulled along in front of the pack. This keeps the terriers' attention on the chase rather than on fighting one another. The first terrier through the hole at the end wins.

As an added safety precaution, the dogs' mouths are fitted with muzzles. This protects not only the other dogs but the handlers and catchers, as well. The muzzles must made as either a plastic basket or from a soft material, and they should not be of the figure-eight variety. In sanctioned events, a muzzle is mandatory.

The course is designed without any turns, and the running area should be about ten feet wide. The race is run on either dirt or turf that provides plenty of traction without injuring the pads of the dogs' feet. The hole at the end is about eight to ten inches wide, which is adequate for a normal-sized JRT to rocket through. The perimeter of the track is defined either by bales of hay or by some type of plastic fencing. The starting box is big enough for six fully grown JRTs and is made from wood, plastic, or another flexible material. After the dogs are loaded into the starting box, a wire or plastic barrier is placed in front of the starting gate and is attached to a release mechanism.

The *official judge* stands at the finish line to record the order of finish and to make sure the run was legal. The judge's decision always is final. The *racing steward* assigns collars, checks all equipment to be sure it is safe and legal, oversees the starting gate, and polices aggressive or fighting terriers. The *starter* makes sure all dogs are properly positioned in the box, opens the gate, and signals the start of the lure by the *lure handler*. The *catchers* remove the terriers promptly from the end box at the finish line to prevent impromptu fights from breaking out.

The steeplechase

Steeplechase races add the difficulty of jumping hurdles to the excitement of the standard race — see Figure 14-1. The jumps are placed at least 20 feet apart, with the final jump being at least 30 feet from the finish line. The terriers must negotiate a minimum of four jumps that are no higher than 8 inches for puppies and 16 inches for grown dogs. The jumps must be flush with the perimeter fencing to prevent the dogs from getting wedged between the side of the jumps and the fence. Competitions usually request that the dogs be fitted with colored collars to help distinguish order of finish and to prevent confusion.

FIGURE 14-1:
The steeplechase
is great fun for
you and your JRT.

WARNING

Don't start training your puppy using any type of jump until he is at least five months old. Puppies' bones are still forming at this age, and they can't take the pressure that jumping puts on their joints. When you do begin, start low and gradually work up to higher obstacles.

Getting ready to race

If racing sounds intriguing to you and you think your dog may enjoy participating in this activity, you will need a few pieces of training equipment and some time to work with your JRT. This is not an event you can just show up and try. It takes a bit of planning, training, and conditioning to be successful, and you need to understand that rarely will a terrier do well in his first few starts.

TRY THIS

Your dog first must be introduced to the lure before any actual race training begins. This is important because your dog needs to get excited about chasing this piece of fur before you can expect him to run his little heart out. Let your terrier catch the lure several times and make it a fun game of tug-of-war so that your dog looks forward to playing with it. You can use a piece of fur, a fuzzy toy, or any other such item that you can safely attach to a 20-foot piece of string and that resembles a fox or squirrel's tail.

Be patient with your dog's performance. Your terrier may need a a significant amount of time to become proficient and comfortable in a race situation, and yelling or getting frustrated only worsens your JRT's attitude toward competition. Always remember that you're at a competition and are being helped by many club volunteers. The more courteous and appreciative you are of their help, the more likely you are to be welcomed back. The competition is supposed to be fun for everyone — dogs included. Approach each competition as an opportunity to improve your JRT's skills, not as a do-or-die situation.

You also need to get your terrier accustomed to wearing a muzzle. Be sure to ask for a plastic basket or *softie* muzzle rather than the figure-eight variety. Tease your terrier with the lure and then run from your JRT while pulling the lure behind you. Your dog still can catch the lure in spite of the muzzle, and you should let him do so from time to time so that he knows he has something to shoot for. School your dog several times until he knows that chasing and catching the lure can be a lot of fun.

WARNING

Be careful not to let your racing JRT overheat while he's wearing a muzzle, which restricts his panting (his built-in air-conditioning system!).

If you're planning to race in the steeplechase division, you need to get your JRT used to following the lure over jumps. You can use something as simple as hay bales or PVC pipe structures, or you can build more elaborate hurdles from wood. Whatever you use, make sure it is safe for your dog and that any solid structures angle away from your terrier as he jumps. Drag the lure over the top of the jump several times to encourage your JRT to jump the hurdle to get the lure. After a brief time, he should be leaping like a pro.

REMEMBER

All this training is valuable for preparing your JRT for the racing division, but none of it takes the place of actual racing experience. Although your Jack Russell may perform famously at home, he may turn into a blathering idiot at the trial himself and may freeze in the starting gate or even run in the wrong direction. With real experience, your dog's racing skills will improve.

Agility Angles

JRT clubs have made it easy for first-time competitors to try their hands at agility training and competition by offering a special division for on-lead competitors. This special class is unique to the Jack Russell breed.

By allowing competitors to keep their terriers on lead, the clubs decrease the feelings of intimidation that often accompany many newcomers to such a complex and difficult sport. It also keeps interest high by providing a controlled and structured environment. By staying on lead to negotiate the course, both terriers and owners can concentrate on the task at hand rather than worrying about an overzealous dog running off and getting into trouble.

Agility competitions are the Olympics of dog training, and hours upon hours of schooling go into a successful agility dog. Because few dog owners have the equipment necessary to train for agility competitions, they often are limited to the time spent at trials to practice working with the required obstacles. On-lead course work gets both the dog and the owner comfortable with the intricacies of each obstacle and provides a means to keep a frustrated JRT under control.

TIP

Patience is the most valuable training tool in agility work. Dogs are asked to jump through tires, to run through tunnels of all shapes and configurations, to maneuver teeter-totters, to walk on a tightrope-like bridge, to swerve through closely spaced poles (called *weave poles*), and to climb up and over a tall A-frame. Not only must they accomplish each and every obstacle successfully, they are timed as well, so they must perform with a high degree of speed.

On-lead courses are offered in both novice and advanced levels. The dogs competing in novice classes are true beginners who literally are just getting the hang of the ins and outs of the sport. The advanced dogs are a bit more skilled but aren't ready to make the jump to the true, off-lead agility classes. After an on-lead Agility Certificate is earned, the terrier must advance to the off-lead agility competitions. After a dog competes in off-lead classes, he's ineligible to return to on-lead competition.

When a dog refuses an obstacle, avoids an obstacle, completes an obstacle out of sequence, knocks down a hurdle, pushes off a rail on a jump, anticipates the beginning of the course, runs under an obstacle, or jumps off and then back on an obstacle, points are deducted from the score. The use of food or toys by the handler, verbal or physical abuse of the dog, the handler touching the dog or the equipment on the course, or the dog eliminating on the course are all grounds for disqualification.

Agility for kids

In the children's division, more emphasis is placed on the child's interaction with her terrier and the child's attitude toward the competition and suggestions made from the judges or coaches. The child also must know the dog's number, the expected course, and how to safely negotiate the obstacles. The judges are far more interested in how the child/terrier team mentally approaches the course than in the actual performance on the course.

AGILITY TRAINING TIPS

Complete training of the agility dog is far beyond the scope of this book, but if, after trying some of the techniques and attending some agility competitions as a spectator, you decide you'd like to give it a serious go, this sidebar can help. You may also want to find some good books geared specifically toward agility training and start mapping out your schooling strategy. Remember that agility training takes a serious time commitment and lots of patience — make sure you're up for it before you invest too much time and money into the sport.

- **Take it easy.** Don't push your puppy into agility work right away. Not only are his focus and concentration levels not fully developed, neither are his bones and joints. Let your puppy grow up first before committing him to agility training.

- **Get in shape first.** Don't kid yourself. Agility is a physical sport for both the handler and the dog. Your terrier must be in peak physical condition to navigate the courses at top speeds, and you have to be equally physically fit to keep up with him. Plan to spend lots of time working on strength and cardiovascular fitness prior to starting serious obstacle training.

- **Start off slowly.** After you and your terrier have reached an acceptable a level of fitness, introduce some of the required obstacles. A low dog walk and small jumps often are some of the easiest obstacles for your JRT to master. If you keep the obstacles close to the ground at first, your terrier is likely to be intimidated should he take a fall or misjudge a jump. As his confidence grows, you can increase the heights of the obstacles and can introduce some of the more difficult equipment such as the A-frame and weave poles.

- **Keep practice fun.** The easiest way to coax a terrier over, around, and through an obstacle is to make a game of it. Terriers love to play and love to eat. Use both of these interests to make your training sessions into one long play session, and your JRT will amaze you at how quickly he can pick things up. If you fall into the trap of getting too serious too quickly, however, your JRT will easily know the difference and become surly and reluctant.

A good agility team is based on trust, commitment, and teamwork. Without these fundamentals, success will be fleeting at best and a distant dream at worst. There should be no pressure to perform and no punishment for hesitancy. There should be only pure joy at a job well done when you and your terrier successfully navigate your first agility course!

Agility courses are perfect for terriers who have a high drive to please their owners. As long as you keep the training fun, JRTs will thrive on the mental challenges necessary to negotiate the obstacles, and they will use their natural proclivity for speed to whiz through the courses. Not only that, they also are wicked fun to watch!

Teamwork at its best

If you're interested in training for this complex sport, first master all of the basic training discussed in Chapter 8 as well as the more advanced commands found in most obedience training books. Agility is a sport that requires extreme concentration and focus from both you and your JRT, and you must spend long hours working together until you're working as a team. Because of this, dogs under one year of age aren't eligible to compete in agility classes.

Contact several trial organizers and ask whether they will be holding agility classes. Attend as many agility trials as possible to introduce your terrier to the required elements and to perfect his skills on each one.

Remember that you can't use the leash as a crutch. The organizers don't allow you to drag your dog through the obstacles, nor can you use fear or intimidation to coerce your dog into submission. You can't navigate the obstacles yourself to show your terrier how it's done, nor can you chase your dog through an obstacle. In other words, you must willingly work together as a team to be successful in this sport!

Chapter **15**

Dealing with Special Concerns

I n spite of the efforts of responsible Jack Russell breeders to rid the breed of all genetic problems, some disorders still pop up from time to time. Under JRTCA rules, veterinary examinations and photographs are necessary to register a dog. These practices have helped shore up the breed's gene pool. Nonetheless, inherited health issues continue in JRTs, in part due to irresponsible breeding.

General Genetics

This section discusses some of the more common problems found in the breed. Please understand, however, that this is not an all-inclusive list, and it shouldn't be used as a guide to diagnosis. Always seek your vet's advice for any symptom or problem you may encounter in your JRT. (Dogs with these disorders shouldn't be bred.)

» **Cardiomyopathy:** *Cardiomyopathy*, an abnormality of the heart muscle, can result in *lung edema* (water in the lung), weakness during exercise, and sudden death. This defect is difficult for the average owner to detect, but if you notice your JRT having trouble after a walk or a run in the park or if you hear her wheezing when she breathes, explore this possibility.

>> **Cerebellar ataxia:** *Cerebellar ataxia* is a neurological disorder resulting from degeneration of the cerebellum's cortex. The degeneration can progress steadily and cause a stagger in the dog's gait. If your terrier appears wobbly on her feet or disoriented from time to time, this disorder could be the cause.

>> **Cryptochidism:** *Cryptorchidism* is the failure of one or both testicles to descend into the scrotum. The testicle is retained in the abdomen or inguinal area, and it may slide in and out of the scrotum. You can easily detect this problem because your male terrier will appear to have only one testicle in the scrotum or will alternately have two and then one, depending on the day. Although this isn't a life-threatening problem, it is best to neuter a terrier born with cryptorchidism. A cryptorchid dog may be more prone to cancer.

>> **Hernias:** *Hernias* occur when a one of the dog's organs or tissues protrudes through a body wall. The most common of these are the *inguinal* hernia and the *umbilical* hernia. These occur when a portion of the intestine falls through the scrotal opening or through the umbilical opening. You will notice a bulge in the dog's stomach or scrotum that looks like a growth. Take your dog to a veterinarian immediately.

>> **High toes:** The term *high* toes or *short toes* applies to a condition in which the toes of the front feet are shorter than normal in a full-grown terrier, giving the appearance of toes that don't touch the ground. This occurs primarily on the front feet, but it has been seen on hind feet, as well. Although not a debilitating defect, it is considered a breeding fault.

>> **Hydrocephaly:** *Hydrocephaly* results from an accumulation of fluid in the brain, and it causes the brain to degenerate. The afflicted dog often becomes disoriented or runs into objects while walking. Sadly, dogs with this condition don't usually live long. For those who survive, treatment often is ineffective. Hydrocephalic dogs often are euthanized.

>> **Legg-Calve-Perthes disease:** *Legg-Calve-Perthes* (also called Legg-Calve) disease is a septic *necrosis,* or degeneration, of the head of the *femur* (the thigh bone). It usually doesn't manifest itself until a puppy is at least six months old, and it can result in progressive rear-leg lameness. It primarily affects small breeds. If you notice that one of your terrier's legs looks different than the other three or that one is particularly susceptible to becoming sore, this disease could be causing the problem.

>> **Lens luxation:** *Lens luxation* is a fairly common inherited disease of the eye in which one or both lenses become partially or completed dislocated from their normal location behind the cornea. In the case of complete dislocation, the lens will be painful and the eye will look red or opaque. Lens luxation, if left untreated, can develop into glaucoma (covered in the following section).

The condition usually manifests itself later in life and should be treated as soon as it is diagnosed to prevent blindness. This condition seems to be relatively common among terriers and particularly among Jack Russell Terriers.

» **Patent Ductus Arteriosus:** *Patent Ductus Arteriosus* is caused by the failure of the fetal vessel between the aorta and the pulmonary artery to close at birth, causing heart murmurs, weakness, and even death. Special care must be taken of dogs with this condition because they are susceptible to heart failure when exercised even moderately. Surgery for this disorder can be quite effective, especially if performed when the dog is young. This is a problem that can't be diagnosed unless the dog is examined by a veterinarian.

» **Progressive neuronal abiotrophy:** *Progressive neuronal abiotrophy* (or ataxia) causes tremors and a lack of coordination in dogs and is caused by degeneration of the cerebellum's cortex responsible for coordinating movements. As a result, a dog develops a staggering gait and becomes unable to stand or even eat.

» **Von Willebrand's disease:** *Von Willebrand's disease,* also referred to as *vWD,* is a common, inherited bleeding disorder that manifests itself through abnormal platelet function. Symptoms include ongoing bleeding of the gums and nose, bloody urine, prolonged bleeding during estrus or after the birth of a litter, and excessive bleeding after surgery or by a slight nick while trimming your Jack Russell's nails. It is caused by an insufficient von Willebrand factor, a blood protein that binds platelets to blood vessels.

Continued bleeding in humans is nothing to laugh at, and it is no laughing matter in the case of your Jack Russell Terrier, either. If you notice that your JRT has a tendency to bleed easily or that bleeding continues for a significant amount of time after a small nick or cut, notify your veterinarian and ask for his or her advice. Mention the fact that your terrier bleeds easily and that the bleeding is difficult to stop.

The disease usually attacks purebred dogs, although mixed breeds also can be affected. The good news is that it isn't as common in JRTs as in other breeds. The bad news is that it can crop up from time to time, and it is serious enough to warrant testing if you suspect your terrier may be a victim. It is important to test for vWD early on, and many experienced and responsible breeders have their breeding stock tested prior to breeding. Breeders often advertise their litters as having been tested for

Disabilities Demystified

Some JRTs suffer from sensory disorders. With the right treatment and/or care, most disabled dogs can live a long and happy life.

WARNING

A Jack Russell suffering from diminished loss of hearing or vision can become irascible when startled. Don't get angry with your dog if she doesn't respond immediately to your commands. She may simply not be able to hear or see you. Give your dog the benefit of the doubt before assuming she's just cranky!

>> **Deafness:** Deafness isn't uncommon in Jack Russells, and it can occur in one (*unilateral*) or both (*bilateral*) ears. It often is possible to detect bilateral deafness in young dogs. A *Brainstem Auditory Evoked Response* (BAER) test can be performed on puppies as young as five weeks old; the test monitors the puppy's brain's electrical impulses. Most responsible breeders advertise their stock as being BAER tested and clear.

>> **Glaucoma:** Untreated *glaucoma* is a serious problem that can lead to partial or total blindness if not quickly addressed. The pressure from fluid built up within the eye can crush the retina's cells and can cause damage to the iris and the cornea. Symptoms include a dilated pupil, cloudiness in the cornea, an increase in the size of the blood vessels in the eye's white portion and pain causing the dog to paw at or rub at her eye. For more information about eye-related disorders, contact the Canine Eye Registration Foundation (CERF). This organization is an excellent resource that is dedicated to the public's education about canine eye disease. CERF can provide considerable information about eye disease and about breed-specific eye problems.

Elegant Elders

You and your dog are headed for your daily walk. As you bend down to hook up her leash, you suddenly notice that her muzzle looks grayer. As you trot down the street together, her gait is slower and she seems to tire more easily.

You may not have noticed the passage of time, and the realization that your beloved terrier is getting older can be difficult to accept. As your dog ages, there are some things (covered in the following sections) that you, as a loving, caring owner, can watch for.

Fitness for seniors

Jack Russell Terriers are known to retain their pep far longer than many breeds. As a general rule, they age very well. Even the feistiest terrier, however, is likely to become less active over time. Your dog may sleep more and may seem a bit stiff after lying down for extended periods of time. She may exhibit signs of arthritis and may prefer to sun herself in the backyard than chase a Frisbee.

You must exercise your older JRT using any physical activity she enjoys. If you don't, her internal workings will slow, and age will creep more quickly into her joints. Her toenails will grow longer and will need to be trimmed more often. She also may gain weight and begin to appear more lethargic. Keep in mind, however, that reasons other than age may keep your dog from being active. If your dog suddenly favors the rug near the fire than a walk down the street, and if she greets you with less than enthusiasm as you approach with leash in hand, your vet should check her for arthritis, heart problems, lameness, or any number of problems that may account for her lack of energy.

I can't overemphasize the importance of exercise to help your older dog keep her weight down, her joints more flexible, her heart strong, and her *joie de vivre* (joy of life) intact. Part of a Jack Russell Terrier's charm is her bright, happy nature and her willingness to play. Just because she doesn't voluntarily leap and jump like she used to doesn't mean she won't enjoy a good game of fetch or a walk around the park. Encourage as much activity as your terrier can comfortably handle. If you keep your older Jack Russell active, she will reward you with many good years of love and companionship.

Weather woes

Cold weather can take its toll on your older JRT, and you may find your dog buried under the comforter on your bed during the winter months. Avoid extreme temperatures because your older dog will find it more difficult to adjust to extreme cold or heat. If you must take her to or live in a chilly climate, a heating pad and a warm sweater will help. And be very careful not to get her overly chilled.

Conversely, if Death Valley is your destination, make sure your Jack Russell has plenty of fresh water to drink and keep the air conditioner on cool. Never leave your elderly JRT — or any dog! — unattended in a car on warm days, no matter how short a time you plan to stop. The temperature in a car can escalate in minutes to well over 100 degrees, and this can quickly cause a life-threatening situation for your dog. Surely you've encountered the 2-minute pit stop that turned into a 15-minute expedition. Although this usually is just a cause of aggravation and frustration, with your beloved JRT waiting in the sweltering car, you could be signing her death warrant. Resist temptation and either have your passenger take your JRT for a walk while you're in the store or bypass the stop altogether.

The elder appetite

A diet change can be traumatic for an older dog, so forget about introducing her to Beluga caviar or Camembert. An older dog needs a balanced diet consistent with her current needs. Choose a good-quality dog food recommended by your veterinarian or one that your dog enjoys and stick with it. Two or more feedings a day are better than one big meal. It isn't unusual for an older dog to eat more slowly and sometimes pick at her food, but if you notice a marked change in her eating habits or a sudden gain or loss in weight, call the vet to make sure your dog isn't ill. A sick dog often stops eating or drinking altogether, and this can lead to rapid weight loss and dehydration.

Overweight Jack Russell Terriers are rare because they are so active, but this can become a problem for a senior dog who doesn't exercise as much as she used to. The added pounds are likely to tax her heart and joints. Just because your older JRT begins packing on the pounds, however, doesn't necessarily mean she's eating too much. Weight gain also can be the result of illness or disease rather than a slower metabolism. If arthritis develops, a heating pad, aspirin, or a drug prescribed by your vet can help.

Other aging issues

Sight and hearing decrease as your dog ages. You dog may experience a hardening of the lens, making her eyes look a blue-gray color that nature never intended. This doesn't significantly affect her vision. In addition, *cataracts* resulting from diabetes can make your older Jack Russell's vision blurry. Both of these problems easily can be corrected with the help of surgery.

Older dogs often develop an unpleasant odor as the result of poor dental hygiene, impacted anal sacs, ear problems, or kidney dysfunction. Investigate any malodorous and unusual smells. Breath mints won't help here, but a vet's thorough cleaning of accumulated tartar, usually done under anesthesia, may. Although this routine is easily performed on younger dogs, your older JRT may be at a greater risk from being put under. A general checkup is advisable prior to subjecting your dog to anesthesia. Your vet can inform you of the options available to solve the problem without taking too much risk with your old-timer.

WHEN AT LAST WE SAY GOODBYE

Parting is such sweet sorrow and, despite all your tender, loving care and your JRT's long lifespan, the time inevitably will come when your best efforts, your love, and your vet's most devoted care no longer can prevent the advance of time nor remedy its ravages. You will have to say goodbye to your old loyal friend.

It is a cruel fact of life that dogs don't live as long as humans. Tough as they are, they eventually succumb to either illness, injury, or old age.

Talk with your vet and decide on an appropriate time to say goodbye. If your dog is in pain and the vet feels that further treatment will prolong that pain, it's kindest to ease any obvious suffering by having your dog humanely euthanized. You can and should enlist your vet's help when making this very personal and difficult decision. By preventing your Jack Russell from further suffering, you're giving her the gift of freedom from pain, and she will appreciate your sacrifice.

Don't be ashamed or embarrassed to cry at the loss of your Jack Russell. It's normal after the many years of love and companionship you and your JRT have shared, and you have earned the right to grieve for your terrier. Ignore the insensitive comments of people who say, "It was just a dog." If they have never owned a pet, they don't know what they have missed and can't relate to what you're feeling. Instead, try to surround yourself with friends and family who also knew and loved your JRT. Know that, as much as it hurts, you will feel better with the passage of time.

The time may come when you want to purchase another JRT. A new dog can never replace the one you lost, but she can give you a second opportunity to love a member of that very special breed. Take your time, however, before entering into another friendship. You may need to grieve and to resolve your feelings before you can open your heart to another Russell. Remember that each terrier is unique in her own wonderful way. The new JRT may bring you different joys than your lost friend did.

5

The Part of Tens

If you're interested in becoming involved in your JRTs registration possibilities, this part fills you in on the ins and outs of the current registries, including requirements for registration, breed standards, and how to go about obtaining registration papers for your JRT. This part also offers suggestions on traveling with your JRT, finding pet-friendly lodging, packing your pooches suitcase, and considering some health matters before traveling with your dog.

And if you're out surfing the Net and want to find out more about JRTs, this part gives you loads of sites and resources to help you find out more.

Chapter **16**

Ten Things to Know about the JRTCA and the AKC

The two primary methods of registering your Jack Russell are through the JRTCA and the AKC. This chapter shares more information about what each organization has to offer.

The Jack Russell Terrier Club of America (JRTCA)

The JRTCA (Jack Russell Terrier Club of America) is a club devoted to Jack Russell Terriers. Members and those selected to run the organization are JRT lovers who want the breed to remain healthy and happy.

The JRTCA opposes registration with the AKC and UKC

Working in concert with the Jack Russell Terrier Club of Great Britain (JRTCGB) and the Jack Russell Terrier United World Federation (JRTUWF), which is a world-wide organization, the JRTCA opposes registration of Jack Russell Terriers with the American Kennel Club (AKC) or any other all-breed registry. The JRTCA fears that, should the breed be registered by these organizations, the history and purpose of the dog will be sacrificed for show-ring appeal. The organization doesn't want Jack Russells to fall victim to the fate of other purebred breeds and succumb to genetic and mental defects and the effects of inbreeding.

Likewise, the JRTCA opposes registration with the United Kennel Club (UKC). The UKC, like the AKC, registers a variety of breeds. The UKC began accepting Jack Russell Terriers for registration in 1992 against JRTCA's advice and wishes, but many owners supported the move. As JRTs become increasingly popular, it is inevitable that additional registries will spring up to offer even more registry choices to JRT owners. It is important to keep in mind, however, that you are the final judge and jury when deciding what registry and clubs are right for you. Everyone is likely to have an opinion, but you are the one who has to live with your decision.

The JRTCA believes Jack Russell Terriers have maintained their integrity of form and function by avoiding inbreeding and by keeping out serious faults since the late 1800s. Many other breeds either no longer resemble their ancestors or the resemblance has considerably faded. Opponents, however, cite the ever-increasing physical problems within the breed (see Chapter 15) as proof that these standards simply aren't working.

Like Jack Russells themselves, JRTCA proponents are a tenacious group and are devoted to preserving their opinion of what the breed should be. Another of the group's goals is to demand the highest standards from Jack Russell breeders. The organization also seeks to inform and educate the public about the breed, and it urges newcomers to investigate the JRT's idiosyncrasies before buying one.

The JRTCA registers JRTs one by one

The JRTCA's breed registry is unique in that each application for registration is judged on the dog's own merits. The registration of the dog's parents doesn't automatically ensure that the offspring will be accepted for registry. A JRT can't be registered under JRTCA guidelines until he's one year old so that his teeth, height, and other aspects of his growth and maturity can be evaluated. The terrier then is either accepted or denied based on his own unique merits or faults.

To register a dog with the JRTCA, certain documents must be obtained. First, an original veterinarian's certificate (not a copy) designed specifically for Jack Russell Terriers is issued by a licensed vet and is signed within 30 days of application. The certificate must state that the dog has been examined and that he is free of genetic defects such as hip dysplasia or epilepsy. If your dog has been neutered or spayed, an appropriate certificate attesting to this fact from an accredited veterinarian can be accepted in lieu of a vet certificate.

As of January 1, 1997, a full four-generation pedigree issued by the breeder (with five generations preferred) also must accompany the application for registry. Any dog who shows significant inbreeding is not accepted for registration. A three-generation pedigree is required to register a spayed or neutered dog. The owner of the sire also must supply a stud certificate that verifies the breeding of the stud to the dam of the dog to be registered.

Clear photographs of the dog (front, back, and side views) must be submitted to evaluate his conformity to breed standards. The photos should be taken on level ground and should clearly show the dog's body, legs, and feet. The front photo should clearly show the ears, head, and legs to evaluate *conformation* (the dog's structure, breed characteristics, and movement). Each photo must be signed by your veterinarian as truly representing the dog examined. A new veterinarian certificate form was implemented in January 1996, and the registry no longer accepts registrations submitted on forms older than January 1995.

If your Jack Russell Terrier was purchased from a breeder who has a kennel registered with the JRTCA, the kennel name can precede your chosen terrier's name. If the breeder isn't JRTCA registered, the kennel name can't be included as part of your dog's registered name. The club recommends that breeding stock be registered prior to being bred. Although the JRTCA can't endorse or recommend a specific breeder to prospective buyers, it supplies a JRTCA informational packet containing an extensive breeders' directory that lists more than 90 breeders throughout the United States. The listings include a picture and a description of the JRTCA breeders, all of whom must subscribe to the Breeders' Code of Ethics.

Any dogs not accepted into the registry are certified, which means the owner receives a certificate and the dog is listed in the registry files as certified but not registered. The JRTCA prides itself on turning down dogs unsuitable for registry due to genetic defects and other physical flaws, thus attempting to protect the Jack Russell's future and physical integrity by keeping serious faults from being propagated within the breed. Many critics, however, claim that these faults are creeping in regardless of the registration policy and feel that the AKC is as discriminating in their stock, thus fueling the controversy between these registries.

The JRTCA operates a Russell Rescue

One of the most important and valuable services that the JRTCA offers is its Russell Rescue's placement service for abandoned or displaced JRTs. This labor of love is supported by people who care and are concerned about all Jack Russell Terriers and their welfare. Many people make the mistake of purchasing a Jack Russell because their kids think they're cute and want "a funny little dog like the one on TV," only to discover that the dog's personality and traits don't fit in with the family's lifestyle. Many of these dogs end up in a rescue placement service, some living with several families before finding a permanent home.

The donations received by Russell Rescue are used for spaying and neutering, vet services, vaccinations, temporary housing, and other needs of abandoned terriers. Russell Rescue cautions potential adoptive owners that many rescue dogs have special problems that must be recognized and addressed prior to making a commitment to a rescued Jack Russell.

Even if you find that this type of dog isn't for you, all Russell Rescue homes need the support of the general public to continue their work. The public can help by:

>> Making donations of dog supplies

>> Offering free veterinary services for spaying and neutering

>> Paying for costs involved in shipping a dog to his new home

>> Providing advertising services

>> Providing dog-grooming assistance

>> Contributing funds for educational programs to instruct the public about the personality of the Jack Russell Terrier

The American Kennel Club (AKC)

The AKC (American Kennel Club) registers a wide range of dog breeds and bases those registrations on the registration of a litter's parents, not on the health of each puppy in the litter. In addition to registry, it offers a variety of services.

The AKC registers many breeds of dogs

The offspring of dogs registered with the AKC automatically are eligible for registration. AKC registry alone, however, doesn't ensure quality because neither the dog being registered nor his parents are examined to determine their suitability for registration. In addition, the AKC doesn't require blood-typing or other proof to verify that the resulting litter is indeed the product of the claimed parents. All reputable breeders, however, strive to ensure that their stock closely conforms to the quality of perfection demanded by their particular breed standard, and they work hard to maintain accurate breeding and registration records.

Dogs with limited registration, usually dogs from one registered parent and one unregistered parent or a dog that, for any number of reasons, shouldn't be bred, can compete in all AKC events (except conformation competitions — see Chapter 14) and have access to all AKC educational and informational services. Fully registered dogs can compete in all AKC-sanctioned activities.

If a dog is sold as AKC registerable, it means the puppy or dog is eligible to be registered but the registration papers have not yet been sent in. The buyer should receive a registration application form, which the seller fills out first. He should then give it to the buyer, who completes it and sends it on to the AKC with the appropriate registration fee. All required signatures should accompany the registration application. Upon receipt and process of this registration — and provided all information furnished is complete and correct — the new owner receives an AKC registration certificate.

The AKC researches pedigrees

A female dog can mate with several males if facilities aren't property regulated and controlled, thus making the dam's offspring of doubtful origin. Remember that female dogs ovulate each and every time they're bred. It is very possible for a bitch to produce puppies from more than one sire. Thus, it is possible that the sire listed on a puppy's registration papers is not the true father of the pup.

Although the AKC has taken steps to prevent this type of registration misuse, it unfortunately still occurs. You, as a buyer, should be aware of these practices and should protect yourself from this type of fraud whenever possible. The AKC will often investigate and even revoke the registration of a litter if research reveals that the inspected puppies or adult dogs don't resemble the breed under which they are registered or if the puppies have traits that couldn't possibly have occurred as a result of mating the two claimed dogs.

The AKC helps with ownership issues

The AKC has stringent rules regarding ownership, change of ownership, ownership of dogs by commercial organizations or corporations, naming of dogs, contracts to spay or neuter, and stud and dam breeding contracts.

If a dog with AKC papers is sold or given away to a shelter or a rescue organization, the documentation must be marked "void" and returned to the AKC. It can't be given along with the dog. Likewise, if you buy a puppy or an adult dog from a pet store, the AKC requires that the store have transfer forms available for AKC-registerable puppies purchased from private owners or breeders. These transfer forms must accompany the puppy at the time of the sale. If they aren't available, it is the pet store's responsibility to supply the buyer with the puppy's breed, sex, color, correct markings, date of birth, litter number (if available), sale date, and the names of the sire, dam and breeder. Such puppies can't be registered in the store or kennel's name. Only individuals can own dogs, and the dog's ownership chain must be traceable.

The AKC offers ingenious identifications

Among its many services, the AKC sponsors a Companion Animal Recovery program that operates 24 hours a day. The program provides identification and recovery services by utilizing a central database that records identification numbers for dog owners who choose to use a permanent form of identification. Anyone trying to locate a dog identified with a *microchip* implanted under his skin or a *tattoo* on his skin can contact the AKC's Companion Animal Recovery program and give it the dog's identification number.

Any animal shelter or participating veterinarian who finds a lost dog can scan him to see if a microchip has been implanted. As of September 1998, more than 280,000 dogs have been enrolled in this program and more than 10,000 lost animals have been reunited with their owners, representing a 100 percent success rate of recovery.

Although tattooing also offers the advantage of permanent identification, it can be less effective than a microchip over time. Tattoos can become blurred (especially if the dog grows and the tattoo stretches) can be difficult to find on a dog's body, and are sometimes difficult to trace back to the owner.

Microchips and tattoos don't guarantee that your dog won't get lost or be stolen, but it gives you an advantage in the recovery department. Permanent identification is important and should be seriously considered, especially considering the amount of money invested in a registered dog compared to the very modest cost of the procedure. Note that microchip identification isn't required by AKC for either registration or participation in AKC events.

The best way to have your dog tattooed or implanted with a microchip is to consult your veterinarian and have him or her perform the procedure. If you decide to use a microchip, an AKC Companion Animal Recovery enrollment form and collar tag are provided. The form should be filled out and sent to the AKC immediately. If your dog already is identified with a microchip implant other than the one used by the AKC, you can call the AKC's toll-free number to ask for an enrollment form. This also can be done over the Internet, and the fee is reasonable.

The AKC extends research resources

One of the most widely used AKC services is its library — one of the largest libraries in the world devoted solely to dogs. The library was established in April 1934, and it presently contains around 16,000 volumes. It includes bound periodicals, foreign and domestic stud books, art, literature, juvenile books, videos, stamps, and bookplates. A collection of *AKC Gazettes*, the official AKC publication, and stud books are available to people involved in research.

The AKC library is an archive for anything about purebred dogs, and it covers topics ranging from origins and breeding to practically any dog-related item of interest to dog owners. It provides assistance, guidance, and direction to anyone interested in advancing the welfare and understanding of purebred dogs.

Its main categories include individual breeds, training, breeding, and care. The library subscribes to more than 250 periodicals and newspapers worldwide that provide information about sporting, hound, working, terrier, toy, nonsporting, and herding breeds.

THE JRTAA REGISTERS JRTs FOR THE AKC

The Jack Russell Terrier Breeders Association (JRTBA), now called the Jack Russell Terrier Association of America (JRTAA), is cooperating with the AKC in registering Jack Russell Terriers. In 1987, the organization began restructuring itself to meet the AKC's guidelines. In 1992, it also incorporated the AKC's structure and layout. Its by-laws also follow the AKC format.

Although the AKC officially recognized the Jack Russell Terrier as of November 1, 1998, the AKC's secretary advised that, effective March 1999, the AKC has decided to no longer accept open registrations for Jack Russell Terriers. The AKC also stated that all future dogs wanting to become AKC registered must come from AKC-registered parents, and the breeder must register the litter with the AKC. In other words, if you want an AKC-registered puppy, you must purchase a puppy with previously registered AKC parents or from an AKC-registered litter.

The library's primary function is to respond to its members' requests for information not available from other AKC departments. Its staff attempts to obtain the necessary information to enable dog owners to make selective and informed choices regarding their specific area of inquiry. If you decide that you want to own an AKC-registered Jack Russell, you can access this library through your membership.

The AKC sponsors the Canine Good Citizen Program

The AKC also sponsors the American Kennel Club Canine Good Citizen program. This is a certification program that tests a dog's behavior in daily situations in a relaxed and positive atmosphere. Dogs demonstrating that they are reliable members of the family and are members of the community in good standing receive an AKC Canine Good Citizen certificate.

The program is fun as well as beneficial and is not competitive in nature. In addition to creating a new bond with your dog, it also represents a test of your dog's good manners and his desire to please you. Both purebred and mixed-breed dogs are accepted. Tests include acceptance of strangers in a friendly situation, sitting quietly and allowing petting in the presence of his owner, appearance and grooming, and walking on a loose leash or through a crowd. Other tests involve the sit and down commands, coming when called, reaction to strange dogs or other distractions that cross his path, and the ability to be left alone when necessary.

The Canine Good Citizen test is administered at a variety of locations including kennel clubs, obedience clubs, training facilities, parks, recreation centers, and community colleges. Anyone interested in this program can obtain forms and kits directly from the AKC if your group, club, or interested organization of dog owners wants to coordinate an event.

The AKC established the Canine Health Foundation

The AKC's Canine Health Foundation was established in 1995 and was started with a $1 million endowment. Its purpose is to support and encourage research to foster healthy dogs, particularly in the area of genetics. The AKC and its Canine Health Foundation have been leaders in funding research to identify and solve genetic problems currently affecting dogs worldwide. The AKC Canine Health Foundation has enabled researchers to create vaccines such as the one developed for the parvovirus, which kills puppies and young dogs of all breed types.

Dogs can suffer a variety of ailments that lead to severe health problems and death. Although some diseases, such as arthritis or cancer, are similar to those found in humans, others are breed-specific. The work of researchers such as Dr. George Brewer of the University of Michigan, for example, has resulted in the identification of a gene that causes copper toxicosis in Bedlington Terriers. This discovery has the potential to completely eliminate this particular disease. A recent infusion of foundation funds has been earmarked for identifying genetic markers for various doggy diseases. Work currently is in progress in the hope that such research will help prevent potentially fatal diseases from being passed on to future dog generations.

The AKC awards scholarships

The AKC awards scholarships to outstanding college students who have in some way substantially contributed to the world of purebred dogs. In 1998, 47 such scholarships were awarded to deserving students based on financial need, academic performance, future potential, and the student's involvement with purebred dogs. Students must be enrolled full time in an accredited college of veterinary medicine.

Chapter **17**

Ten Ways to Take a Vacation with your JRT

Traveling with your Jack Russell Terrier is a bit like traveling with children. You can't just open the door, hustle your dog into the car, and drive off. You need to prepare, plan, and anticipate, but none of it needs to be overwhelming. If you plan properly, your vacation with your JRT can be downright fun!

Go to the Vet Before You Leave

Approximately two weeks prior to your trip, take your dog to the vet for a complete examination. Be sure all her vaccinations are current. If there is any chance you may be traveling in areas where your dog may be exposed to Lyme disease or another disease particular to a certain area, notify your veterinarian so that he or she can recommend the appropriate vaccine. Flea treatment also is a good idea, preferably a good topical or feed-through treatment (see Chapter 10) that will continue to work throughout your trip.

If you plan to do any hiking or camping, make sure that your dog is physically strong enough to manage the terrain and the altitude. It isn't a good idea to take a dog on a long, strenuous hike if she is younger than 18 months old because of the strain it may place on developing joints and limbs. Check with your vet to make sure your terrier is physically up to the challenge of this type of activity. If you take your dog hiking in a heavily wooded area, make sure you check her daily for ticks at the end of the hike.

Plan Ahead

Whether traveling by car, motor home, or plane, the trip can be enjoyable and rewarding and will open new horizons to you and your dog. It also can be a nightmare if you haven't planned properly. Before you leave, you need to establish which hotels, motels, resorts, and beaches don't allow dogs. Don't wait until you get there and are tired, hungry, and in a less-than-receptive mood to be told that your pet is unwelcome.

Pack Your Pooch's Suitcase

Bring along items that are familiar to your dog, such as her favorite blanket, bowl, chewies, and toys, and make sure to pack plenty of dog food. Remember that changing your dog's food type can be stressful on your dog even at home, let alone on the road. This is especially important if your dog is on a special diet or if she eats a type of dog food that may be difficult to find along the way.

A leash or a retractable lead is a must when stopping at a rest stop, park, or beach, as is a well-fitted harness or collar. Be sure to place your terrier on her leash *before* you let her leave the car to keep her from dashing out of the car before you're ready. Jack Russells move at the speed of lightning, and there is nothing more terrifying and time-consuming than trying to locate your dog in an unfamiliar park or rest area or near a freeway where she can be injured or killed.

A crate is a must for your dog to travel in. Not only is it a sanity saver, it ensures your dog's safety, as well. A dog bouncing around in a car can injure herself during a sudden stop and can even cause an accident if she distracts the person driving by jumping on his lap, sticking her head out the window or jostling around. Remember to line your dog's crate with a soft towel and secure food and water bowls so they don't spill or move around. Aside from the actual travel time, you also will find the crate particularly useful when staying at a motel. Your terrier is more likely to feel at home and relaxed in her crate and is less likely to cause a disturbance.

A "doggy travel kit" is an invaluable addition to your list of travel supplies and should include the following:

>> A topical antibiotic

>> Eye drops

>> Tweezers for thorn and splinter removal

>> Pepto Bismol for stomach upsets

>> Gauze for wound dressing and cleansing

>> A flea comb

>> A brush

>> A penlight for night excursions

>> Plastic or another type of bags for poop disposal

>> Shampoo

>> Plenty of paper towels or towelettes

>> An extra blanket and sweater for nippy weather

>> Your dog's rabies and vaccination certificates and license tag

>> Temporary ID tags with the addresses and phone numbers of your scheduled stops along the way

REMEMBER

Expect your dog to be a good traveling companion. Basic obedience training is the key — your dog should be able to sit and lie down when told, come when called, get in and out of her crate without a fuss, stand quietly when leashed to go out or unleashed to return to her crate, and ride quietly along without distracting the driver with untimely or uncontrollable barking.

Take a Travel ID

Make sure your dog is wearing a collar with an identification tag stating your name, address, and phone number. It also may be helpful to carry a picture of your Jack Russell Terrier for identification purposes in case she gets lost or stolen. A tattoo or a microchip (see Chapter 16) is also an excellent source of permanent identification, although it is tougher for anyone who finds the dog to decipher how to contact the owner. A tag can tear away from the dog's collar or become worn or illegible, whereas a chip or tattoo will always remain on your pet. Err on the side of caution, and have a tag on your dog's collar in addition to a microchip or tattoo ID.

Travel Comfortably by Car

If your dog never has been in a car before, take her on short trips in her crate to condition her for the journey. This way, you can take precautionary steps such as bringing an old towel along should your dog become carsick. Likewise, if your dog never has been crated before and you plan to use a crate while traveling, allow plenty of time before the trip to get your pooch accustomed to traveling in a confined area.

WARNING

Don't force your dog into the crate. This may frighten her and make her reluctant to try again. Instead, tempt the dog into the crate with a treat or a toy and make the experience pleasant rather than stressful. Better yet, use the crate at home as a safe, pleasant place for your dog to go, and she will be comfortable sleeping there while traveling. (Just keep in mind that your dog should be crate-trained long before traveling!)

If this is a summer trip, traveling in the early morning or evening is best to avoid the midday heat. Several water jugs often can be lifesavers if your car breaks down and you must cool off your pet. The water jugs also can double as drinking water for your dog in case you find she has a sensitive stomach and is susceptible to changes in water.

Don't leave your dog loose and unattended while traveling, even for a short period of time. It only takes a second for a "dognapper" to do his dirty deed and walk away with your pet, or for your terrier to free herself from her leash if tied improperly.

REMEMBER

Exhibit the same courtesy and standards while traveling with your dog as you do when walking with her in your own neighborhood. Remember to bring plastic baggies or other containers to pick up any messes made on hotel grounds and make sure your dog minds her manners while in the hotel room.

WARNING

Never leave your pet unattended in a car with the windows rolled up. A locked car without ventilation can become a death trap or can cause serious injury to your dog. It only takes a few minutes for the temperature in your car to reach dangerous levels. If you have to make a stop with your terrier in the car, make sure it is for a very brief time.

Make Rover's Home Away from Home Comfortable

Prior to booking your reservation, inquire whether the motel or hotel of your choice accepts dogs, what the additional charge is, if any, and what management's policies are for animal guests. Ask about pet exercise areas and try to reserve a room at the end of the hall and away from busy areas such as the pool or ice and vending machines. Be sure to remind management when checking in that you're traveling with a dog.

Many books on the market list facilities that welcome pets, such as the following:

>> *20,000 Hotels, Motels and B&Bs That Accept Pets in the U.S. and Canada*

>> *The Pets-R-Permitted Pet Travel Directory or On the Road With Your Pet*

In addition, many Web sites such as those that follow, also are dedicated to pet travel:

>> `www.petswelcome.com`

>> `www.traveldog.com`

>> `www.dog-lovers.com`

>> `http://members.spree.com/sip/wolfsong/PET_FRIENDLY.htm`

>> `www.dogfriendly.com`

>> `www.inns.com/pets.html`

>> `www.petfriendlytravel.com`

>> `www.collierem.org/pets`

>> `www.travelpets.com`

>> `www.jcn1.com/mbamford/pets_allowed`

The lodging industry is in constant flux, and a hotel or motel's policies vary depending on sale of facilities, changes in management, and the like. The number of establishments that accept pets seems to be decreasing, yet a respectable number still accept and welcome your dog, providing you follow their rules regarding noise control and places where the dog can relieve herself. A well-behaved dog is usually welcomed back whereas one bad apple can ruin the experience for everyone.

Many hotels and motels cater to dog owners. Try to find lodging at a place that not only tolerates dogs but welcomes them. Many times these facilities offer extra features for your four-legged friend, and it's nice to know ahead of time what you can expect.

As soon as you check in, take your dog for a "nature walk" in a quiet, calm area to give her a chance to relieve herself, sniff around a bit, stretch her legs, and get used to her new environment. Avoid busy areas where your terrier could be overly stimulated and make sure to clean up after your pet if she leaves a mess behind.

Some motels catering to dog owners have special places where dogs can relieve themselves and play. Most, if not all, expect you to clean up after your dog. Even if the area is fenced off, keep your pet in her harness or collar and on a retractable leash so you can promptly intervene if a fight with another dog breaks out or in order to keep your dog from wandering away.

Upscale hotels that welcome dogs may have dog walkers on staff who can take your dog for a walk while you're out. The service is pricey, but it is worthwhile if you can afford it to ensure that your Jack Russell is exercised and entertained while you're away. One hotel in Massachusetts offers a special "Cause for Paws" weekend package to pet owners who want to enjoy a luxury getaway weekend, and it contributes some of the proceeds to the Massachusetts Society for the Prevention of Cruelty to Animals.

If you have to leave your dog alone at the motel, make arrangements with motel management or find a one-day boarding facility that can look after her safety and well-being while you go to the zoo, the museum, or on a shopping or sightseeing trip. Remember that many motels won't clean your room unless your dog is crated. This prevents her from frightening or biting a member of the staff and from slipping out the door for a fast getaway when the door is opened for housecleaning. If it is summer and the room is very warm, leave a window open, preferably one in the bathroom, for fresh air and ventilation. Better yet, turn the air conditioner on low to ensure your terrier's comfort while you're away.

If your motel or hotel is receptive to the idea of leaving your dog in the room for a day or for part of a day while you shop or go sightseeing, give her food and water and then take her out for a brisk walk before you leave, making sure she relieves herself prior to returning to the room. Before leaving your JRT behind, play with her for a while, pet her, and then put her in her crate and leave, just as you would if you were home.

Fly Away

Whether you're taking your dog along on a pleasure trip or are shipping a dog to a new home, airplane travel has become increasingly common as a mode of travel for dogs. If your dog is small enough, she may be able to ride in a crate under her owner's seat. This is obviously the preferred choice. If this option isn't available, your dog is required to travel crated in the cargo area.

REMEMBER

Ask the airline you intend to use what choices are available and what type of crate or cage is required. Some airlines require you to use their crates.

The crate should be secured (bungee cords work well for this or you can tape the crate shut if cords are unavailable) to prevent the door from accidentally opening in flight and to deter unauthorized individuals from accessing your pet. Line the crate with a soft blanket or a rag that your Jack Russell is familiar with to make her more at ease and to ensure easier cleaning if the dog soils or wets the crate. A few chewy toys or rawhide bones should keep your dog company. Be sure to insist that the appropriate personnel give your dog plenty of water. Don't, however, feed your dog just prior to the flight. Doing so may contribute to an upset stomach during the trip.

REMEMBER

In the winter, many airlines won't fly your pet if the temperature is below 45 degrees. You should know, however, that summer is the worst time for your dog to fly because of high temperatures in the cargo area. Sadly, some dogs have dehydrated or even died in an overheated cargo space.

Never ship your dog in the heat of the day, especially in the summer. Find out whether a late-afternoon or evening flight is available and, if the flying schedule allows it, book a nonstop flight to minimize the chances of your terrier getting lost, stolen, or caught during plane changes or delays. Summer is the worst time for your dog to fly, especially if your dog can't accompany you under your seat. Waiting on overheated tarmacs before being loaded for the flight has proved fatal to some dogs.

TIP

A frozen bowl of water traveling with your dog is an excellent way to provide a water supply to your Jack Russell Terrier. It prevents water from spilling into the crate and drenching your dog's bedding, but it still provides plenty of cool water throughout the trip.

Things can and do go wrong during a flight. Your dog is away from you and from your control, so you must take care to minimize problems by doing everything you can to ensure your dog's comfort and safety. Courtesy and respect toward individuals who will be handling your dog during the flight also go a long way toward gaining a cooperative attitude on the part of the airline employees.

If you're traveling on the same flight as your dog (and you should), find out ahead of time where your dog will be unloaded. (Animals aren't placed on luggage conveyors.) You also may want to inform the pilot or the flight attendant that you're traveling with a dog. They often can let you know when your dog's crate has been loaded in the cargo area. This should be done each time you change planes — hopefully, your dog will change planes, as well.

Be prepared and informed because no one cares as much about your terrier as you do. Don't assume the airline "is in charge and things will be just fine." Many flights have carried pets on board without a problem, but there also have been instances in which an owner's prompt intervention saved a dog's life.

Leave Your JRT Home

What happens if you have to go out of town and can't take your terrier with you? You have several options available to you.

Home alone

First, if you're going to be gone only a short time (such as a day), you can leave your dog alone with plenty of food and water and an open doggy door. This is assuming you have a JRT who is safe to leave alone without coming home to a refurbished interior.

You may want to have a friend or relative come over and check on your dog, play with her a bit, and take her for a walk. Don't expect friends and relatives to act as a substitute for you, however. Trust me, your terrier will know the difference.

Pet sitting

Another choice is to hire a pet sitter. If you hire someone whom you don't know but has been recommended, be sure to check his references prior to entrusting your JRT to his care.

A stay at the kennel

You may choose to find a good boarding kennel to keep your dog for the duration of your trip. Kennels range from plush to austere, and naturally, you want to choose one that's right for your dog and still fits your pocketbook. Don't be tempted to sacrifice good care to save a few bucks. After all, you're leaving one of your family's beloved members behind. You should feel comfortable that her welfare and safety will be well tended to while you're away.

Inspecting the kennel

Examine the facilities yourself before dropping your dog off. Don't take a friend's word that they are "absolutely wonderful with Buffy." Make an appointment to visit several kennels midweek because Mondays and Fridays are their busiest times for dropping off or picking up dogs. If you're refused an appointment or are limited as to when you can visit or what they will show you while you're there, take this particular kennel off your list and go on to the next one.

At the very least, the kennel should be clean and well ventilated, and the boarded dogs should appear happy and healthy. The chosen kennel also should have indoor-outdoor runs that are cleaned and disinfected daily and that are suitable for your dog to exercise in. Keep in mind, however, that *all* runs can't be clean *all* the time. Make allowances for a few droppings here and there, provided the kennel is free of unpleasant urine or old feces smells. This should be apparent even as you're chatting in the front office with the kennel manager. There is a big difference between a freshly cleaned kennel with only a few scattered dog droppings and the smell of old urine and decay, so use your nose to guide you. Make sure the runs are adequate in size and offer plenty of protection from the weather.

If the kennel looks to be in disrepair or has dirty floors, stale food, or no food at all, and if water bowls look none too clean, leave and go elsewhere. Also look at the facilities where your dog's food will be kept and inquire about feeding schedules. Ask what type of dog food the kennel provides and whether you're able to provide your own food, should you choose to do so. If your terrier is *free-fed* at home (a bowl of food is available all day long), ask if they will continue the practice while you're away and clarify any special dietary needs your terrier may have. Your dog's bedding should be off the cold concrete floor and her regular eating schedule should be continued, just as if she were home.

TIP

Ask specific questions about basic costs and what entails an additional charge. Your questions should include the following:

>> Will I be charged extra if the staff needs to administer worming or other necessary medication to my dog?

>> What is the staff's training? Do they love animals? Are they caring and compassionate?

>> Can staff members recognize my dog's needs and address an illness or other emergency by acting promptly?

>> What arrangements have been made for emergency care and with what veterinarian?

>> If I want my dog housed in a separate run and I am willing to pay extra, is this an available option?

>> Is someone at the kennel 24 hours a day?

Don't be shy about asking for references and talking to the staff yourself.

Some of the better kennels are booked far in advance, so make sure to reserve space in a timely fashion when you decide on one that suits your needs and desires. If the kennel has no room during the time you intend to reserve space, ask to be put on its waiting list and to be notified if a cancellation occurs. It is okay to make multiple reservations with different kennels, but don't forget to cancel any other reservations when a suitable opening becomes available at the kennel that's your first choice. This common courtesy goes a long way toward ensuring that your business will be welcomed in the future.

Leaving your dog in good hands

Bring records of your Jack Russell's medications, vaccinations, and any health problems that the kennel owner should know about, especially if you're boarding an older terrier. You also should leave your vet's name and number with the kennel owner or manager in case your dog gets sick. If she's currently under treatment for a specific ailment, alert the staff.

GETTING YOUR JACK RUSSELL READY TO BOARD

If your dog never has been boarded before, a bit of preboarding training will be necessary. At the very least, your dog should be able to walk on a leash without pulling or struggling, if the staff is expected to take her for a walk. It also is helpful to familiarize your dog with strangers ahead of time if she hasn't been around many people other than the family. Teach your dog to sit quietly when ordered so the staff won't worry about your pet dashing out the door every time she is about to be fed or her dog run cleaned. If you're going to ask the kennel to bathe your dog, teach your JRT to stand in the tub without trying to bite, scratch, or get away from the staff person who is trying to give her a bath or trim her nails.

SURF FOR TRAVEL IDEAS

For Web sites that offer advice, tips, ideas, and strategies for travelling with your pet, visit the following:

- http://www.petswelcome.com
- http://homearts.com/hl/articles/78trav11.htm
- http://jetpets.com
- http://www.netfopets.com/travel.html
- http://aolsvc.travel.aol.com/travel/interest/pets.jsp
- http://takeyourpet.com
- http://www.dogsaway.co.uk
- http://dogfriendly.svwh.net/us/hotel/us.html
- http://www.rovinwithrover.com

TIP

Inform the staff of your dog's quirks or idiosyncrasies. If your JRT is skittish with strangers, say so. If she retreats into a corner and pouts the first few days you're gone, let them know. This will make things easier for everybody all the way around.

REMEMBER

Some kennels offer suites instead of runs, fluffy beds rather than blankets, larger accommodations, and more personalized service. Regardless of these bonanzas, don't expect a kennel, even the very best, to be just like home. Only you can give your dog the care and attention she deserves. You should view the kennel as just an acceptable alternative.

Chapter **18**

Ten Great Web Sites to Visit

Although just a few years ago the Jack Russell Terrier was virtually unknown to all but his enthusiasts, the use of JRTs on television and in films has boosted their popularity dramatically. Currently, thousands of Jack Russell Terrier owners can be found both in the United States and overseas. Obviously, all these folks have something in common — a love for the funny little dog who owns them and a desire to be in touch with people who share their enthusiasm and affection for the breed. If nothing else, it's nice to know other people out there are as crazy as you are for owning one or more of these little terrorists.

With the increase in popularity of the Web and the growing number of Jack Russell Terrier enthusiasts, many new Web sites are dedicated to locating and informing Jack Russell Terrier owners about specific activities, areas of interest, and clubs to bring together JRT lovers and enthusiasts, owners, or prospective owners. Many of these sites also offer information, training tips, and other useful ideas about how to entertain your dog and how to meet other Jack Russell Terrier owners.

JRTCA Official Site

The Jack Russell Terrier Club of America (JRTCA) is the oldest and largest of the registries recognizing the Jack Russell Terrier in the United States. It is geared solely to JRTs (see Chapter 16 for more information) and is focused less on the show ring than on hunting and working terriers.

The Web site of the Jack Russell Terrier Club of America (JRTCA) (www.terrier.com) is particularly valuable to prospective JRT owners. Its home page contains a wealth of links and information about the breed ranging from how to decide whether a JRT is right for you to video clips and worldwide JRT links. It also contains a multitude of stories from other Jack Russell owners about their dogs' antics and odd behaviors. This is a good place to go if you're feeling overwhelmed by your terrier's personality and need to know whether others are having the same problems you are.

Among other things listed on the Web page are reminders of the typical JRT personality — JRTs are very active, they often can be aggressive with other animals and pets, they fare better in a home with a yard, and they must be kept busy and exercised. Most of all, they are social little creatures who don't do well if left alone all day or if ignored for extended periods of time. Both experienced and novice JRT owners can become overwhelmed by the demands a Jack Russell makes on their lives and time, which often is why they give up the terrier, who ultimately ends up in rescue placement.

The Jack Talk Forum offers a long list of valuable topics, problems, and anecdotes from Jack Russell owners who then have the opportunity to read the questions and answers from other JRT owners worldwide. The forum can help people understand that the specific activity, trait, or strange behavior demonstrated by their JRT is often typical of the breed and that they aren't alone in their frustrations. The forum covers a range of topics from the use of electric fences to behavior problems to house-training or excessive barking. Some of these questions and answers are humorous, some are informative, and all are valuable. You're bound to find a topic that parallels your own experience with your individual terrorist, and you may even get the answer to a question or concern that you've wondered about.

WARNING

Another valuable feature offered by the JRTCA Web page is the Advice section that covers topics ranging from how to join JRTCA to a question-and-answer section addressing the most frequently asked questions of Jack Russell owners. Keep in mind, however, that these resources reflect the JRTCA's viewpoint and don't represent the views of other registries. Ultimately, only you can make the decision as to which registry you want to join. It is up to you, and only you, to use all the information available from a variety of sources to make your own, personal, educated decision.

The American Kennel Club (AKC)

With the recent introduction of the Jack Russell Terrier into the ranks of the American Kennel Club's accepted breeds, many JRT owners are curious as to the standards required of this new registering entity and the benefits and drawbacks of this registry versus those that have been in place for a long time. As of this writing, the AKC is currently not accepting any outside registrations (those of dogs produced from non-AKC-registered parents). It is, however, still accepting inquiries about the AKC in general and about JRTs specifically. The AKC can be reached on the Internet at info@akc.org and you can view its requirements for registration on its site at www.akc.org/breeds/recbreeds/jrt.cfm. You can also contact the Jack Russell Terrier Association of America (JRTAA), the AKC-recognized parent breed club for the Jack Russell Terrier in America, at www.jrtaa.org/index2.html.

JRT Classifieds

If you're looking to purchase a JRT and aren't sure where to start, check out the Canine Connections Classified Web site. This site, at www.cheta.net/connect/canine/breeders/jackruss.htm, offers dogs for sale as well as breeders and dogs at stud.

Another great JRT classifieds site is Breederweb.com. While offering information on all breeds, this site also has a section devoted strictly to JRTs and offers an on-site search engine for a JRT breeder near you. The address is http://breederweb.com/dog_detail.asp?breedId=320

Dirt-Dog.com

The Dirt-Dog.com Web page also lists JRT clubs in certain areas of the country and in some foreign countries. This page can be found at www.dirt-dog.com/clubs/index.html. It's a good source for local, regional, and national terrier clubs, and it often lists schedules and planned events for these clubs.

The Dog Zone

The Dog Zone currently lists JRT clubs in Arizona, Georgia, Ohio, Virginia, and British Columbia (Canada). You can access its Web page at `www.dogzone.com/clubs/jackruss.htm` and get information and a list of contact persons' names, addresses, and e-mail addresses.

Canine Connections

The Canine Connections Web site at `www.cheta.net/connect/canine/breeders/jackruss.htm` features U.S. breeds and kennel clubs by state and by breed as well as an index of information about clubs, pet products, recipes, breeders, and so on. This is a good all-around site for people in search of additional information about dogs in general.

The English Jack Russell Terrier Club of America, Inc.

The English Jack Russell Terrier Club of America, Inc. is the newly formed official registry for the short-legged Jack Russell Terrier. This club is dedicated to establishing recognition as a division of the breed. Because this type of JRT isn't preferred by the other registries, this new registry provides recognition and registration possibilities that were previously unavailable to these dog owners. With the increased popularity of this smaller, more compact Jack Russell, this is the place to meet and talk with other small JRT owners. If you own or are contemplating purchasing a short-legged JRT, you may want to contact this organization for its list of clubs and trial schedules at `www.engjackrussellterrier.com`.

Other Organizations

The following are other organizations devoted to Jack Russell Terriers:

» Jack Russell Terriers Online is an international site that acts as a gathering place for all international JRT owners. It features pictures, articles, and information of interest to Jack Russell fans. Visit the site at `www.jackrussells.com/jrtinfo.html`.

>> For information on Jack Russells in Canada, try Dogs In Canada at `www.dogsincanada.com/breeds/jack_russell_terrier`.

>> For information on JRTs that have adapted to snow, the Jack Russell Terrier Club of Switzerland may be of interest (`www.jackrussell.ch/englisch/home_eng.htm`).

>> The Western Australian Terrier Club is a home for Russell friends down under (`www.iinet.net.au/~siberian/watc.html`).

>> The American Working Terrier Association encourages trials and activities to promote the working aspect of the terrier. Visit it at `www.Dirt-Dog.com/awta/index.shtml`

Appendix

Recommended Reading and Resources

In addition to the many Internet sites provided in Chapter 18, numerous books and magazines are marketed for Jack Russell lovers.

Magazines

The following magazines are aimed at JRT owners:

>> *True Grit* magazine, the official publication of the JRTCA (Jack Russell Terrier Club of America), is included with any JRTCA membership. It lists new clubs and activities and keeps members abreast of issues and information that affect them and their dogs. Find out more by visiting www.terrier.com/jrtca/truegrit.php3.

>> *Down to Earth,* the official publication of the AWTA (American Working Terrier Association). Find out more at www.dirt-dog.com.

>> *Parson's Nook,* the official publication of the JRTAA (Jack Russell Terrier Association of America. For more information, visit www.jrtaa.org.

Books

The Barnes and Noble (www.bn.com) and Amazon (www.amazon.com) Web sites contain extensive listings of books that pertain to specific breeds or training, medical reference, genetics, or any specific activity such as obedience trials, hunting, and working. In addition to books specifically about the Jack Russell breed, general books can help when training, grooming, and trying to decide whether you're interested in breeding your JRT. Many of the medical-care books provide helpful information that dog owners can use when their own veterinarians are unavailable or when immediate attention is necessary on the way to the vet's office.

The following are just a few of the books on market that specifically target Jack Russell Terriers:

- Chapman, Eddie. *The Working Jack Russell Terrier*. Dorchester, Dorset, England: The Dorset Press, 1985.

- Coile, Caroline D. *Jack Russell Terriers: Everything About Purchase, Care, Nutrition, Behavior and Training*. Hauppauge, NY: Barron's Educational Series, Inc., 1996.

- Jackson, Jean and Frank Jackson. *Parson Jack Russell Terriers: An Owner's Companion*. Crowood Press, 1991.

- James, Ken. *Working Jack Russell Terriers*. Bedford, PA: Hunter House Press, 1995.

- Kosloff, George and Raymond S. Vena. *Guide to Owning a Jack Russell Terrier: Puppy Care, Grooming, Training, History, Health-Breed Standard*. Neptune, NJ: TFH Publications, 1996.

- Nicholas, Anna Katherine. *Jack Russell Terriers*. Neptune, NJ: TFH Publications, 1996.

- Plummer, D. Brian, *The Complete Jack Russell Terrier*. New York: Howell Book House, 1980.

- Romaine Brown, Catherine. *The Jack Russell Terrier: Courageous Companion*. New York: Howell Book House, 1998.

- Romaine Brown, Catherine. *The Jack Russell Terrier: An Owner's Guide to a Happy Healthy Pet*. New York: Howell Book House, 1996.

- Valentine, John. *Pet Owner's Guide to the Jack Russell Terrier*. Seven Hills Book Distributors, 1997.

Index

neutering, 30, 80
 benefits of, 131
 terrier trials and, 166
newborn babies. *See also* children
 flea sprays and, 126
 preparing your dog for, 69
 puppies and, 68–70
"no" command, 62, 82
 basic description of, 99
 dealing with unwanted chasing using, 109–110
 overuse of, 99
 puppy aggression and, 113
 timing of, importance of, 88
nursing dogs, 126, 136

O

obedience training. *See also* commands
 accentuating the positive in, 90
 basic description of, 85–100
 charting your progress with, 89
 classes for, 88–89, 100
 consistency in, 87, 90, 98, 100
 diversionary tactics and, 99
 equipment, 89–90
 establishing boundaries, 86–88
 goals, setting, 88
 handling negative behavior with, 98–99
 the importance of repetition to, 91
 the importance of timing to, 88
 sessions, length of, 90
 setting rules, 85, 86–88
 staying focused on, 88
 teaching commands, 89–97
 using your dog's name during, 90
obedience trials, 167–168
older dogs
 adoption of, pros and cons of, 43, 45
 feeding, 135, 138–139, 182
 fitness for, 181
 potty training and, 44, 141
 weather and, 181–182

oleander, 63
omnivores, 134
otitis, 161

P

packs
 hierarchy of, 86
 separation anxiety and, 111
paint thinner, 63
parainfluenza, 122
parasites, 128–129, 161
parks, 151
Parson Jack Russell Club, 23
parvovirus, 122
pastern, 22
Patent Ductus Arteriosus, 179
patience, 34–35, 43, 90, 174
paw(s)
 cracked, 146
 high toes and, 178
 injured, 123, 156
 licking, 123
 protecting, on the beach, 145
 protecting, on winter walks, 30
 thorns in, 123
 ticks and, 127–128
pedigrees, 40, 50, 189, 191
penlights, 199
Pepto Bismol, 199
perfection, 18–21
personality. *See also* temperament
 appreciating your dogs, 32–33
 information, provided by breeders, 49–50
 obedience training and, 85
 rescued dogs and, 45
 traits, that make good pets, 41–42
 pet sitting, 204
pet stores, 56
PetFriendlyTravel Web site, 201
PetsWelcome Web site, 201, 207
philodendron, 63

vaccinations, 121–122, 197
  boosters, 122
  for puppies, 121–122
  records/certificates, 50, 199, 206
veterinarian(s). *See also* vaccinations
  bedside manner of, 120
  certificates from, 189
  fees, 121
  phone numbers, accessing, 123
  traits of good, 119–121
  visiting, before going on vacation, 197–198
vision, 182–183. *See also* eyes
vitamins, 134–138
vomiting, 64, 123–124
Von Willebrand's disease, 179

W
water, 66, 68, 82
  bowls, 136, 203
  bringing, on outings, 144, 148
  hemlock, 63

weather, 30–31, 153–156, 181–182
Web sites
  ten great, 209–213
  travel advice, 201, 207
weight gain, 135–137, 181
weight loss, 137, 182
Western Australian Terrier Club, 213
wheelbarrows, 65
whipworms, 128–130
winter, 153–156. *See also* climate
withers, 22, 24–26, 166
wounds, 122
wrapping paper, dangers of, 64

Y
yards, fenced, 30–31, 43
yeast infections, 161

Z
zap attack, 60
zinc, 146

About the Author

Deborah Britt-Hay has been breeding, training, and laughing at Jack Russell Terriers for the past nine years. She received her first JRT as a wedding present from her husband, Mark. As a nationally accomplished trainer of Arabian, Hackney, and dressage horses, Deborah found that her spunky Jack Russell fit right in with both her clients and her horses. She enjoyed her female so much that a mate was soon purchased, and the Hay household has never been the same.

Both dogs — Annie and Bubba — travel with Deborah and her horses to various shows across the nation. She rarely is found without one of her trusted terriers by her side. Intent on breeding just a few puppies with good conformation and temperament, Deborah and her husband breed only one litter each year, and most of the puppies end up in her clients' households. "It's great to see them so often, to watch them grow, and to know I am providing a few great family dogs that are dearly loved," Deborah says of her litters. "Now we have a whole herd of our Jack Russells at the barn!"

Deborah and her husband live in Southern California with their young daughter, Taylor. Her previous book, *Horse Training Basics: An Indispensable Guide to Beginning Trainers,* was published in 1994. She currently is working on a mainstream suspense series with her co-writer and mother, Nicole Bentley. As Deborah says, "I love to write and I love to teach, so now I have the best of both worlds!"

About Howell Book House Committed to the Human/Companion Animal Bond

Thank you for choosing a book brought to you by the pet experts at Howell Book House, a division of Wiley. And welcome to the family of pet owners who've put their trust in Howell books for nearly 40 years!

Pet ownership is about relationships — the bonds people form with their dogs, cats, horses, birds, fish, small mammals, reptiles, and other animals. Howell Book House/ Wiley, understands that these are some of the most important relationships in life, and that it's vital to nurture them through enjoyment and education. The happiest pet owners are those who know they're taking the best care of their pets — and with Howell books owners have this satisfaction. They're happy, educated owners, and as a result, they have happy pets, and that enriches the bond they share.

Howell Book House was established in 1961 by Mr. Elsworth S. Howell, an active and proactive dog fancier who showed English Setters and judged at the prestigious Westminster Kennel Club show in New York. Mr. Howell based his publishing program on strength of content, and his passion for books written by experienced and knowledgeable owners defined Howell Book House and has remained true over the years. Howell's reputation as the premier pet book publisher is supported by the distinction of having won more awards from the Dog Writers Association of America than any other publisher. Howell Book House/ Wiley, has over 400 titles in publication, including such classics as *The American Kennel Club's Complete Dog Book*, the *Dog Owner's Home Veterinary Handbook*, *Blessed Are the Brood Mares*, and *Mother Knows Best: The Natural Way to Train Your Dog*.

When you need answers to questions you have about any aspect of raising or training your companion animals, trust that Howell Book House/Wiley has the answers. We welcome your comments and suggestions, and we look forward to helping you maximize your relationships with your pets throughout the years.

Howell Book House Staff

Dedication

I'd like to dedicate this book to the two special Jack Russell terriers in my life, Annie and Bubba, and to my beautiful daughter, Taylor. If it weren't for them, I'd would never truly experience the hysterical antics and blind love and devotion they freely offer to me every day. I hope that through this book, their influence in my life will last a long, long time. Thank you for being my friends and companions, and my one-and-only flesh-and-blood.

Author's Acknowledgments

I want to take a brief moment to thank a few people whose support, encouragement, and suggestions were an integral part of this book's success. Thanks to my personal editor, Nicole Bentley, who made sure chapters were as good as they could get prior to sending them to my publisher. Thanks also to the staff at Wiley who gave it a chance as a *For Dummies* book and who, through its pages, allowed me to amuse and inform present and future JRT owners. Unending thanks to Dr. Sandra Singleton, the breeder who introduced me to this wonderful breed. If not for you, my family never would have known the laughter, joy, and frustration of being owned by JRTs. Thanks to the many friends and horse-training clients who generously offered pictures, stories, and ideas to help make this book unique. And special thanks to my husband, Mark, and to my daughter, Taylor. Their needs often took a back seat so I could provide this guide to all of you. You are all very special parts of my life, and words alone cannot express my appreciation for you.

Publisher's Acknowledgments

Project Editors: Tere Drenth, Kelly Ewing
Senior Acquisitions Editor: Scott Prentzas
Editorial Manager: Pamela Mourouzis
Editorial Administrator: Michelle Hacker

Production Editor: Mohammed Zafar Ali
Cover Image: © Jelena Matvejeva/EyeEm/ Getty Images